The
Undies
Book

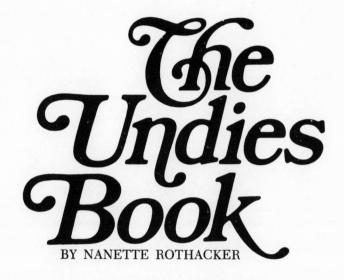

The Undies Book

BY NANETTE ROTHACKER

Charles Scribner's Sons

New York

A Gladstone Book

Copyright © Gladstone Books, Inc. 1976

This book was designed and produced by Gladstone Books, Inc.
Project illustrations by Blaine Saunders
Diagrams by Carol Hines
Victorian Valentine Undies designed by Kathleen Moore
Ski Snuggies designed by Susan McMahon

This book published simultaneously in the
United States and in Canada—
Copyright under the Berne Convention

1 3 5 7 9 1 1 13 15 17 19   I/C   20 18 16 14 12 10 8 6 4 2
Printed in the United States of America

Library of Congress Cataloging in Publication Data

Rothacker, Nanette.
  The undies book.

  "A Gladstone book."
  1. Underwear. 2. Lingerie. 3. Bathing suits.
I. Title.
TT670.R83   6464'2'04   75-41522
ISBN 0-684-14605-3

Contents

Introduction

Making your own undies is fun, easy, and really saves money. Once you have learned a few simple techniques, you will be able to make all kinds of undies, and the possibilities then are endless. You can make up your own patterns, adapt ours, add your own touches—appliqués, embroidery, lace, fancy cam stitches—and buy the most luxurious fabrics available. Or you can recycle fabrics from your old undies, from your threadbare silk shirts, from last year's lace evening dress. Only the imagination limits; this book will supply all the clues.

With very little practice, you will be able to complete any of the projects in this book within an hour's time. You don't need to be an expert seamstress either. One thing that makes lingerie sewing so easy and fun is that lingerie doesn't require the exacting fit that outer wear does—in almost all cases, it has a softer, looser fit. And, if you make a mistake sewing a seam, you can usually just cut it off and sew another one—no bothering about having to rip it apart.

Because a number of the fabrics that you've seen used to make up commercially manufactured undies are not yet widely available in fabric stores, the fabrics we've called for in the projects—and that we discuss in the fabric section—are more limited than we'd like. Nor have we included the really expensive, beautiful fabrics because one of the purposes of this book is to help you save money—and lots of it. The other is to encourage you to view undie making as a craft, as an expression of what you yourself would like most next to your skin—and using costly materials often has the effect of inhibiting creativity and experimentation. After you've become familiar with the basic techniques of undie making, you will no doubt naturally begin seeking out the China silks and the real needlepoint laces—and, by then, you'll be able to work with them with confidence.

Fortunately, nylon tricot, the basic knit material used in making lingerie, is now readily available in nearly all fabric stores and in a veritable rainbow of solid colors and exciting prints. So, your undies can still be as colorful and as different as you desire and for a fraction of the cost of store-bought undies. They will also wear longer and fit better. The projects included in this book range in price from approximately seventy cents for the string bikini to less than four dollars for the long half slip.

As you use the patterns in this book, keep in mind that nearly any one of them could be used for making your own beachwear simply by substituting a swimwear fabric—which means even more money saved. You could also turn some of the full slips or half slips and camisoles into summer sundresses, evening wear, or sleepwear by changing fabrics.

In other words, as you work your way through the projects in this book, let your imagination run free. Completely.

Section 1
All About
Making
Undies

About Fabrics

When shopping for undie fabrics, look for fabric stores that specialize in knits and lingerie fabrics and notions. Familiarize yourself with all the types of materials available. Instead of *looking* through a fabric store, "feel" your way through. With a little practice, you will be able to tell by the softness, pliability, and stretch of the various fabrics whether or not they would be suitable for undies.

There are, of course, materials other than the traditionally used nonwoven knits that are suitable for undie making, such as the polyester-cotton blends, the lightweight rayons and rayon blends, and the polyester crepes. For very special lingerie, try working on your own with the beautiful fabrics—the gauzes and batistes, the organdies and voiles, the silks and satins.

Keep in mind that the fabric requirements given in each project of this book specify the amounts needed to make that particular project—they do not reflect the widths that various fabrics are manufactured in. The reason for this is that the same fabric—for example, tricot—may come in several different widths, depending on the manufacturer, making it impossible to specify standard widths.

Knit Fabrics

Most fabrics that you use for making undies should be preshrunk. Wash the fabric in the washing machine or by hand, using warm water, and dry it in a warm dryer. This precaution is especially important for knit fabrics, as knits may shrink anywhere from 2 to 7 inches per yard, depending on whether they are of cotton, nylon, or a combination of cotton and synthetic material. Cotton knits will shrink the most—anywhere from 4 to 7 inches. If the knit you buy is labeled "preshrunk," wash it anyway—it will probably shrink some more.

When you are preshrinking knit material, it is important to let it cool before you handle it. Otherwise, you may stretch the yarns and, thus, the fabric. Either leave it in the dryer or remove it carefully in a bundle and let it rest for several hours or, better still, overnight. This procedure will allow the yarns time to relax naturally.

Adding fabric softener to the wash water will help reduce the static electricity that is so often a problem with synthetics. However, no garment should be subjected to regular washings with fabric softener—if it is, its life may be shortened considerably because fabric softener chemicals tend to weaken fabric fibers.

Use a flat surface for cutting knits, and don't allow the fabric to hang off the edge of the cutting surface, for this will stretch the fibers. Cut with sharp scissors. Do not use pinking shears; they encourage knits to ravel.

Tricot. Lingerie tricot is made from nylon yarns and comes in light, medium, and heavy weights. The medium-weight tricot of 30–40 denier is the most common weight used in making undies. Tricot can be found in most fabric stores in solid colors that range from the demure pastels to the vibrant blues and reds and yellows. It is also available in prints. Although it is manufactured in widths that range from 44 inches all the way to 108 inches, the solid colors tend to be 108 inches wide and the prints, 44 inches wide.

The crosswise grain of tricot has the greatest amount of stretch. Be sure to lay out the pattern pieces on the tricot so that the stretch will go *around* the body. A hint: Tricot is easier to cut when it is laid out single thickness than when it is folded double, because it tends to slip and crawl on itself. When you need to cut two of a particular pattern piece on a single layer of tricot—or any other fabric, for that matter—be sure to flop the pattern before you cut the second piece so that you will have both a right and a left pattern piece.

It is difficult to tell the right side of tricot from the wrong side by just looking at it. However, when it is pulled with the stretch, or crosswise grain, it will curl to the right side. Once you have made that determination, mark the right sides of each tricot piece you have cut for a project with a strip of transparent tape. This bit of preparation will prove most helpful when you are constructing the garment.

Lycra spandex, or power net. This fabric has a two-way stretch capability and is available in three weights—light, medium, and heavy. The medium weight, which is the easiest to find in fabric stores, is used for girdles and bras. The lightweight version is suitable for undies that need less control, such as body bras and briefers. Referred to interchangeably as power net, Lycra spandex, and just Lycra, this fabric comes in various colors and prints and does not need to be preshrunk.

Before cutting Lycra, determine the right and wrong sides of the material. The right side will have a slightly raised texture whereas the wrong side will feel smooth to the touch.

Lycra differs from other undie fabrics in that the greatest amount of stretch is the same as the grain of the fabric. Both run parallel with the selvage. When you are placing pattern pieces on Lycra, you must be sure that the grain line and the greatest amount of stretch will go *around* the body (Diagram 1). If you are in doubt

Diagram 1

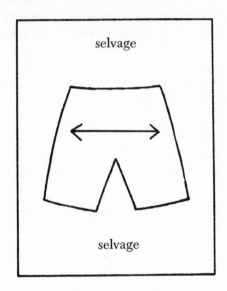

as to whether you have really found the grain line, stretch the fabric with your hands until the small holes close—that will be the grain line as well as the greatest amount of stretch.

Fiberfill. Fiberfill, which is usually made of polyester, is a lightweight batting used for padding bras. It can be found in fabric stores carrying lingerie materials and is sold by the yard in most cases. It does not need to be preshrunk.

Lace paneling. Lace paneling is an all-over lace fabric that has been fused to a nylon backing. Generally, it is used to make the decorative outer cups of fitted bras and the support panels of girdles, although you may well find other interesting uses for it. Happily, it comes in a number of colors and can be found in fabric stores that carry the lingerie fabrics. It should not be preshrunk.

Polyester-cotton single knit. This fabric is available in various blends of polyester and cotton or it may be made solely of polyester or cotton. It is used mainly for men's ready-made undershirts. Available in many colors and pattern designs, the lighter-weight, soft single knits are especially suitable for panties. Many women prefer this fabric for panties to nylon tricot because it "breathes" better.

This knit is available in flat and tubular versions. The flat version will have been knitted flat, in a sheet form. Two of its edges will be finished, and it will be available in widths ranging from 44 to 60 inches. Tubular knits will have been knitted in a circular, tube form and may have creases on each side where they have been folded. A tubular knit must be cut on the lengthwise grain—*after* it has been preshrunk—and any creases avoided when you are laying out the pattern pieces, for they are nearly impossible to press out.

All polyester-cotton single knits should be preshrunk, and the pattern pieces should be laid out so that the greatest amount of stretch —in this case, the crosswise grain—goes around the body. If you have difficulty determining the right side of the fabric, stretch it on the crosswise grain and it will curl to the right side.

Nylon and Lycra-spandex combination. This two-way stretch fabric should be approximately 86- to 87-percent nylon and 13- to 14-percent Lycra. Commercially, it is known as Flexknit, but you won't find it under that name in fabric stores. Used primarily for making the natural-look panty girdles and bras, this fabric can usually be found among the swimwear materials. You might also check in the section containing body-suit fabrics. You'll have to read the labels carefully to find just the right combination of nylon and Lycra.

Since this material has Lycra spandex in it, the greatest amount of stretch will be the same as the grain line, which is parallel to the selvage. Be sure to place pattern pieces on it so that the grain—and the greatest amount of stretch—will go around the body.

It is not necessary to preshrink this fabric. Its right side is the shiny, silky side, and it is available in 42- to 54-inch widths.

100-percent nylon two-way stretch. This fabric is a nylon single knit that is very soft, light in weight, and stretchy. It is, therefore, ideal for making up the one-size-fits-all type of undies, such as string bikinis and leisure bras. Because it is often used for swimwear linings, look for it in stores that carry swimwear fabrics. Many body suits are also made of this, so check in that area, too. It is available in various colors and patterns, but it can be difficult to find. The width of the fabric may range from 44 to 54 inches.

Again, the greatest amount of stretch is with the crosswise grain, and the fabric should be preshrunk before you begin working with it.

Cotton knit and Lycra-spandex combination. This fabric should be 90- to 95-percent cotton and only 5- to 10-percent Lycra. It has two-way stretch, and it is very soft and light in weight—the small percentage of Lycra in it gives it more stretch and body. Because it contains Lycra, the greatest amount of stretch will be the same as the grain line and will run parallel to the selvage.

This material is frequently found in commercially made bikinis and leisure bras, but, as yet, it is difficult to find in the stores. It can sometimes be found among the body-suit and swimwear fabrics. The width of the fabric varies from 44 to 54 inches.

Woven Fabrics

There are many woven fabrics that are suitable for undies. These fabrics should also be preshrunk, in the same way as was described for the knits. However, since they do not have the stretch that knits do, it is not necessary to let them rest after drying. They may be taken from the dryer and folded immediately.

Full slips, half slips, and camisoles can be made from such fabrics as gauze, Qiana nylon, polyester-cotton blends, lightweight rayons and rayon blends, and polyester crepes. Since these materials have no stretch, patterns should be cut on the bias to enable the garments to fit better and eliminate the need to insert stretch-knit gussets. The bias-cut full slip and the peasant petticoat are examples of woven fabrics being used for undie making.

Recycling Fabrics

When preparing to make yourself some new undies, don't overlook your old, wornout clothing for fabric possibilities. Bras and panties both can be made from old slips and men's undershirts. The latter, for instance, is excellent for making cotton knit panties. Since undershirts usually wear out around the necks and armholes, whole front and back sections will remain, which will supply plenty of good fabric for a pair of panties.

If you prefer tricot panties but like the inner crotch to be of cotton, an old undershirt again will provide the perfect material.

Tricot panties may be made from old tricot slips, since it's usually the bodice and hemline that wear out first. Old tricot slips will serve just as well for making a tricot bra, of course. You might also recycle a pair of pretty print tricot panties for bra cups.

Here's another idea: If you have an old full slip on which the bodice and hemline lace is a little the worse for wear, cut the bodice off at your waistline and add ½-inch-wide lingerie elastic to the waist. Then cut off the old lace at the hemline and replace it with new. If the slip needs lengthening, choose a wide lace for the hemline—and presto, you have a brand new half slip at practically no cost.

About Tools and Equipment

Sewing Machine

You don't need a fancy sewing machine to make undies. It is easier if your sewing machine has a zigzag stitch, but it is not absolutely necessary in most cases. The exceptions in this book are the panty brief girdle, the body briefer, and the long-leg panty girdle. These should be constructed with a zigzag stitch so that the seams have the necessary amount of stretch and give. (You might try making these projects by sewing three rows of straight stitching on each seam while stretching the fabric as much as possible, but we can't make any promises as to how long-lasting the garments will be.)

Be sure to keep your machine oiled and free of lint. Frequent cleaning is necessary when you are sewing with lingerie fabrics, for they produce a great deal of lint.

Sewing-Machine Needles

To prevent knit fabrics from "running," a ballpoint sewing-machine needle should be used to sew them instead of a sharp needle; the ballpoint needle has been specially designed to separate the yarns of a knit whereas the sharp needle will simply cut through them. A size 9 needle works best on the lighter-weight fabrics.

A regular sewing-machine needle can be used on the woven lingerie materials. A size 9 or 11 needle should be used, depending on the weight of the fabric. In general, the lighter-weight fabrics need the smaller numbered needle.

Change your sewing-machine needle often. A dull needle will cause skipped stitches, especially on tricot.

Pins

Ballpoint pins or fine, sharp, silk pins work best on lingerie fabrics. Again, ballpoint pins are preferable, for they will separate the yarns instead of cutting them. Never sew over the pins! Always remove them as you come to them to keep from dulling and damaging your machine needle.

Thread

A dual-duty extra-fine nylon thread—lingerie thread—works best. The polyester and polyester-cotton threads may be used, but they are not as satisfactory.

Scissors

A pair of very sharp scissors is essential for cutting the lightweight lingerie fabrics. A pair of bent-handle scissors makes the job easier because they allow you to cut the fabric without having to lift it from the cutting surface. Lingerie fabrics will dull scissor blades quickly, so be sure to check them frequently for sharpness. Also, wipe away any lint that collects.

Pattern Paper

Pattern paper can be bought by the yard at fabric stores. There are several kinds available. One type is called Perky Pattern Paper and is made by Stretch & Sew, Inc. Unlike the others, it is made of paper, is 40 inches wide, and is printed with dots that mark off 1-inch squares.

The latter feature will prove most convenient when you are enlarging patterns.

Other types are made of fabric and include Trace-A-Pattern and Do-Sew. Trace-A-Pattern is made by Stacy Fabrics and is 100-percent nonwoven nylon fabric 36 inches wide. Do-Sew is a 40-inch-wide synthetic nonwoven fabric found at Stretch & Sew fabric stores. The fabric pattern papers have the advantages of being very transparent and of not ripping or tearing.

Brown wrapping paper or sheets of tissue paper may also be used for pattern making.

To trace your patterns, use a ballpoint pen or an indelible felt-tipped pen. Both will mark seams as well as grain and stretch lines permanently.

Transparent Tape

Transparent tape makes sewing undies a lot easier and quicker. It has several uses and is easily removed once it has performed its tasks. Because it is difficult to determine the right and wrong sides of many knit fabrics used in making lingerie, it is helpful to place a piece of transparent tape on the right side of each pattern piece as you cut it out. This will save time when you are assembling the garment. Because transparent tape can be written on with ballpoint pen, it is also useful for marking seams. Finally, this tape can be used to hold lace trims in place until they have been sewn to a garment. Pins have a tendency to stretch and pull on fabric and lace, whereas the tape will hold them flat. Then you can sew right through the tape and remove it afterwards or you can remove it as you come to it.

About Patterns

Enlarging and Making Patterns from This Book

To enlarge the patterns in this book, you will need some kind of pattern paper, a ballpoint pen or indelible felt-tipped marker, and a yardstick. The pattern paper that is already marked off in 1-inch squares is the easiest to use (Perky Pattern Paper by Stretch & Sew, Inc.). All you have to do is connect the dots on the opposite edges of the paper to make a grid with 1-inch squares. Of course, you can also use other pattern papers, brown wrapping paper, or tissue paper—just make certain that you have a piece large enough to accommodate the patterns. Then divide the surface into 1-inch squares, using a yardstick and pen.

Now that you have a grid, copy the lines from each square on the pattern in the book—make sure that you copy the lines for *your* size—into the corresponding square on the grid. (Since all the patterns in this book include a ¼-inch seam allowance, do not add any extra when you are making the patterns.)

You can also enlarge a pattern by means of a pantograph, which is an inexpensive device available in art-supply stores. Follow the directions that accompany it. Another means of enlarging is by photostating. Any store that does professional Xeroxing will no doubt have a photostat machine. Simply indicate how much enlargement you wish and, for about a dollar, you will have an enlarged pattern.

If you prefer your patterns to be made of the fabric pattern paper so that they will last longer, simply lay the pattern "paper" over the enlarged pattern pieces and trace the lines showing through. Then cut out the pieces.

After you have enlarged and cut out all the pattern pieces you need, label each with all pertinent information.

Making Patterns from Old Undies

Making your own patterns from old undies can be done simply and ensures a correct fit. This method works for all kinds of lingerie with the possible exception of girdles, which may have been too stretched out of shape to make a proper-fitting pattern. It is not even necessary to rip apart seams of undies that you want to use—simply *cut* them apart at the seams. For more complicated constructions such as bras, it is advisable to cut apart only one half of the bra. The other half will guide you while you are assembling the new garment.

To make a pattern, lay the pieces of the garment you are using out flat on a sheet of pattern paper and trace around each with a ballpoint pen or indelible felt-tipped marker, being sure to add a ¼-inch seam allowance. Add a notch wherever it will help you to put the garment together properly, and be sure to mark the grain and stretch lines. Then cut out the pieces. For very little expense and trouble, you have a pattern for a garment that will fit you perfectly.

Buying Patterns

Most of the large pattern companies now have a limited selection of lingerie patterns. There are also a number of small pattern companies that offer a selection of such patterns. Each pattern usually includes several sizes, each of which is designated by a different color. The correct size pattern is made by placing pattern paper over the commercial pattern and tracing over the lines for the size needed. These commercial lingerie patterns can usually be found in fabric stores that specialize in knit fabrics.

About Fitting Techniques

Since lingerie does not require the exacting fit that outer clothing does, it is, in general, much easier to make. However, there are a few problem areas that should be mentioned.

When making panties with a crotch piece, you may need to alter the width of the crotch, since the crotch piece given is the same size for all pattern sizes. As a rule, the larger a person is, the *narrower* the crotch piece needs to be. You can easily adjust the piece, however, by simply sewing the elastic farther in at the sides of the crotch by the amount that it needs to be narrowed.

To lengthen panties (or slips), cut the pattern apart halfway between the waist and the legs (Diagram 2). Place another piece of

Diagram 2

pattern paper behind the pieces and separate them by the extra amount that is needed. Then tape the pieces in place to the paper behind. This can be done to both the front and the back, as necessary.

To shorten a panty (or slip) pattern, fold out the excess amount halfway between the waist and the legs on both the back and front pieces, as needed (Diagram 3). Then straighten the side seams.

Diagram 3

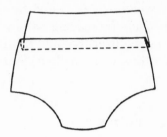

When measuring yourself to determine your correct pattern size, take your measurements while you are wearing a bra and panties. Use a tape measure, and measure around the fullest part of the bust, your natural waistline, and the fullest part of the hips, which is usually about 9 inches below the waistline.

To select the correct pattern size for bra patterns, use the same size pattern as the size you would buy in a commercially made bra. If you are adding padding to the bra, use a cup size that is one size larger than you would normally buy.

About Sewing Techniques

When you are beginning to sew a seam on a lingerie fabric, particularly tricot, be sure to hold the upper thread and the bobbin thread back away from the machine needle. This will help to pull the fabric on through, preventing it from bunching up under the needle.

As a rule, you should never backstitch on lingerie fabrics, especially tricot. For one thing, it usually isn't necessary; for another, if you do, you will find that the fabric will bunch up under the needle. In the few projects in this book where it is necessary to lock stitches, we have noted it. To do it, leave the needle in the fabric, pivot the fabric, and sew back over the seam a few stitches.

Sewing-Machine Stitches and Stitch Techniques

Narrow zigzag. This stitch is used for sewing seams with a zigzag stitch. The stitch length should be set at short length, about 1½ if the stitch length on your machine is marked for 0 to 4 or 0 to 5 or at 15 if the stitch length on your machine is marked by the number of stitches per inch. The width of the stitch should be set at 1½ or 2 to give a narrow zigzag.

Zigzag the seams ¼ inch in from the edge and trim the seam allowance close to the stitching.

Straight stitch. If your machine doesn't have a zigzag, you can still make the undies in this book except for the long-leg panty girdle, the panty brief girdle, and the body briefer, as was noted at the beginning of this section.

Set your stitch length at 2 or 2½ or 12 to 15, depending on the way in which stitch length is marked on your machine. Sew one row of stitching ¼ inch in from the seam edge. Then sew a second row close to the first row between it and the edge of the fabric. Stretch the fabric slightly as you sew in order to give more stretch to the seam. Trim the fabric close to the second row of stitching.

Stretch stitch. Some of the newer machines have a stretch-stitch feature. Although this stitch is not required to make undies, you may use it if you wish.

Rolled seam. This is the seam found on commercially manufactured lingerie that gives it that finished look. It is easy to duplicate at home if your machine has a zigzag stitch. Set the stitch length to short—either 1½ or 15, depending on your machine—and the width to 4 or 5. Then sew along the edge of the seam so that the zigzag goes over the edge of the fabric. Practice first on a scrap of tricot until you can do it easily. You'll be amazed at how little practice it will take.

This type of seam is used most frequently for joining the side seams in panties, slips, and camisoles.

Topstitching. Topstitching is used to give added strength to bras and girdles and to attach elastic and lace to undies of all kinds. It is always done on the right side of the garment.

If you have a zigzag machine, lengthen the stitch length to 2 if stitch length on your machine is marked from 0 to 4 or 0 to 5 or to 12 if stitch length is marked by the number of stitches per inch. The width of the zigzag should be set at about 4.

If your machine doesn't have a zigzag stitch, set the stitch length to 2 or 2½ or 12 to 15, depending on your machine, and sew two parallel rows of stitching.

About Laces, Elastics, and Straps

Laces

Laces that you choose for lingerie should be 100-percent nylon. It is not necessary to preshrink these.

Stretch lace. Stretch lace is a combination of nylon lace and nylon elastic and is available in various widths and colors. It can be bought by the yard in fabric stores that carry lingerie material and notions.

Stretch lace gives a smooth, body-hugging fit to undies and has more stretchability than regular lingerie elastic. Consequently, it is a natural as leg finishing on girdles, as waistband and leg elastic on panties, as top finishing on slips and camisoles, or as straps for slips and camisoles.

The right side of stretch lace is the textured side; the wrong side shows horizontal rows of elastic. To apply stretch lace to undies, lay it on top of the garment so that its wrong side is against the right side of the garment; then topstitch it in place, stretching the lace to fit the garment if necessary. Trim the fabric behind the stretch lace close to the topstitching.

Hemline lace. This kind of lace, which should also be nylon, is available in many widths and colors. It may have one straight edge and one scalloped edge, both edges straight, or both edges scalloped. It can be bought by the yard in lingerie fabric stores.

It is used at the hemline for full and half slips, to trim the bodice tops of slips and camisoles, as decorative inserts on slips and panties, and as appliqués for panties, slips, and bras. The right side of the lace is the raised, textured side.

Lingerie Elastics

Lingerie elastics should be 100-percent nylon. They come in different types and widths and should not be preshrunk. They are available in a variety of colors and can be bought by the yard at fabric stores that have lingerie materials and notions.

Panty or half-slip elastic. This elastic comes in ¼-inch and ½-inch widths and has one edge that is ruffled. The ¼-inch width is used for panty legs and the ½-inch is used at the waist of half slips and panties. It has no right and wrong side.

Plush elastic. This type of elastic has a soft velvet nap on one side. This is the "plush" side and is worn next to the skin. It varies in width and usually has a picot trim on one edge. It is used on both bras and girdles. Some plush elastic has picot trim on both edges; it is used to make bra straps.

Lingerie Straps

Ready-made straps for slips, camisoles, and bras can be bought at lingerie fabric stores. Nylon satin ribbon straps with adjustable sliders can be used for slips and camisoles. Straps made of tricot with an elastic insert or all-plush elastic straps can be purchased for bras. These are available in many solid colors.

If you prefer to make your own straps, there are various types you can make. You can purchase small plastic or metal adjustable sliders to add to your homemade straps if they need to adjust to different lengths. You can also recycle these from old garments. To make straps for certain types of bras, such as the halter bra or the bandeau bra, you will also need four bra slide closures of the hook-on type in order to change the straps from halter to crisscross to straight. These hook-on bra slide closures can be purchased, or you can use those from an old halter or strapless bra that had detachable straps.

Stretch lace straps. This type of strap is simple to make and is very comfortable on slips and camisoles; however, it is not adjustable. To make stretch lace straps, cut two pieces of 1-inch-wide stretch lace 18 inches long. Attach one end of each piece to the back of the slip or camisole, behind the lace trim, and topstitch it in place. Try on the garment and pin the front ends to the front bodice to the length at which they are most comfortable. (More detailed instructions are given with the individual projects calling for this style of strap.)

Plush elastic straps. Plush elastic that is ½ or ⅝ inch wide and that has a picot trim on both edges can be used to make your own bra straps. If you can find plush elastic with the picot trim on only one edge in the color you want, cut the trim off so that both edges are straight. Then cut two pieces of the elastic 18 inches long. Add adjustable sliders and hook-on bra slide closures, following the directions accompanying their packages. (See individual projects for more detailed instructions.)

Self-fabric straps. Since ready-made straps come in solid colors only, this type of strap is particularly nice for bras and slips made from a print tricot. To make this style, cut a strip of tricot that is 36 inches long—this strip must be cut with the lengthwise grain so that the straps don't stretch. The width of the strip should be three times the desired finished width of the strap. Fold the long edge in twice on each side so that the folded edges meet in the center. Press with a

Diagram 4

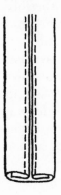

warm iron as you fold. Then stitch down each folded edge (Diagram 4). Cut the strip in half to make two 18-inch-long straps and attach them to the garment, adding adjustable sliders if you wish.

Ribbon straps. Use nylon satin ribbon in any width that you prefer. Cut two lengths of ribbon to the desired length and add adjustable sliders. Attach the straps to the garment by topstitching.

Lace and ribbon straps. Nylon lace in any width can be combined with nylon satin ribbon to make a fancy strap. The ribbon should be slightly narrower than the lace. Place the right side of the ribbon against the wrong side of the lace, centering the ribbon. Stitch down each edge of the lace, thereby attaching the ribbon to the lace

(Diagram 5). The ribbon will show through the lace designs on the finished strap.

Diagram 5

Spaghetti straps. Cut a strip of tricot about 36 inches long and 1 inch wide on the lengthwise grain. Place a string that is slightly longer than the strip of tricot down the center of the right side. Fold the strip right sides together so that the string runs down inside the center of the fold. Stitch one end of the strip closed, catching in the string securely. Then stitch a ¼-inch seam allowance down the length of the strip, being careful not to catch the string (Diagram 6). If you want a flat

Diagram 6

strap, trim the fabric close to the seam. If you want a rolled strap, do not trim it. Pull the string to turn the strip right side out; remove the string by cutting off the stitched end (Diagram 7). Then cut the strip in half to make two straps, and attach them to the garment with top-stitching. A spaghetti bow can also be made from one 18-inch rolled strap by tying the strap into a bow and sewing it to a garment.

Diagram 7

About Trims and Decorations

Lace Trims

To apply lace to the hemline of a slip, place the bottom edge of a length of lace along the lower edge of the slip, wrong side of the lace against the right side of the slip. The bottom edge of the lace may be either straight or scalloped, depending on your preference. Topstitch along the top edge of the lace. Trim the fabric from behind the lace, cutting close to the stitching.

Lace Inserts

To make a lace insert on a slip or panty, tape the lace, in whatever width you wish, to the garment wherever you want to place the insert (Diagram 8). For panties, do this step before sewing the side seams;

Diagram 8

for a slip, do it before sewing the second side seam so that the garment can be laid flat. The wrong side of the lace should be next to the right side of the garment. Topstitch both edges of the lace, and trim the fabric behind the lace close to both seams. For a different effect, leave the fabric behind the lace.

Lace Appliqués

Appliqués made from lace scraps can be sewn to undies before the garments are stitched together. Cut around a design or pattern in the lace, leaving a bit of the lace netting around the design. Experiment by arranging different sizes and different colors of appliqués into various patterns. After you have arranged the appliqués, tape them in place and stitch over the edges with a small zigzag or straight stitch. Cut away the tricot behind the appliqué or leave it as a backing. If you are sewing on the appliqué with a straight stitch and plan to cut away the fabric behind, use two rows of stitching around the edges.

Embroidery

Decorating your undies with embroidery is limited only by the imagination. Names, initials, quotations, animals, hearts, flowers, and geometric designs are only a few of the endless possibilities. Try your hand at designing your own patterns or use any of the hundreds of embroidery transfers and patterns available commercially.

Spaghetti Bows

Spaghetti bows can be used to trim panties, slips, bras, or any other kind of lingerie. Cut a piece of nylon sheer tricot about 6 inches long and ½ inch wide. If your machine has double spool pins, use them to form the loops of the bow. Pull the fabric around both spools tightly and tie it in the middle. Otherwise, hammer two nails about 2 inches apart into a length of board and use the nails in the same way as for the spool pins. Tack the completed bow in place on the garment.

Section 2
Undies
to Make

Project 1
Panty Brief

Making up this basic panty brief pattern is an excellent way to begin saving money by sewing your own undies. Depending on where you buy your fabrics, you can make a pair of these briefs for as little as a dollar and they'll be better made than any you could buy at any price. For one thing, both crotch seams are enclosed on this panty—most commercially manufactured panties have only the front seam enclosed, making them less comfortable to wear and less durable. Also, synthetic fabrics such as tricot do not "breathe" as do natural fiber fabrics and may, therefore, cause skin irritations. For those of you who still prefer the look and feel of tricot to that of cotton, you can prevent this problem by simply constructing a crotch piece that is lined with a piece of polyester-cotton knit.

MATERIALS NEEDED:

⅝ yard nylon tricot *or* polyester-cotton single knit, 44 inches wide
small piece polyester-cotton single knit, for crotch lining (optional)
1 yard lingerie waist elastic, ½ inch wide
1½ yards lingerie leg elastic, ¼ inch wide
nylon lingerie *or* polyester thread

TOOLS NEEDED:

pattern paper
scissors
transparent tape
ballpoint pins
#9 ballpoint sewing-machine needle

PROCEDURE:

1. Wash the tricot to preshrink it. Then measure your hips to determine your size according to the chart below.

| *small* | *medium* | *large* |
| 34–36 inches | 36–38 inches | 38–40 inches |

On the pattern paper, enlarge to size all three pattern pieces (page 17), transfer any pattern markings, cut out the pieces, and label them.

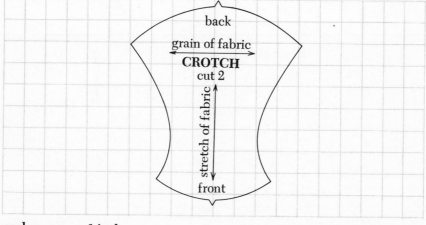

each square = 1 inch

each square = 1 inch

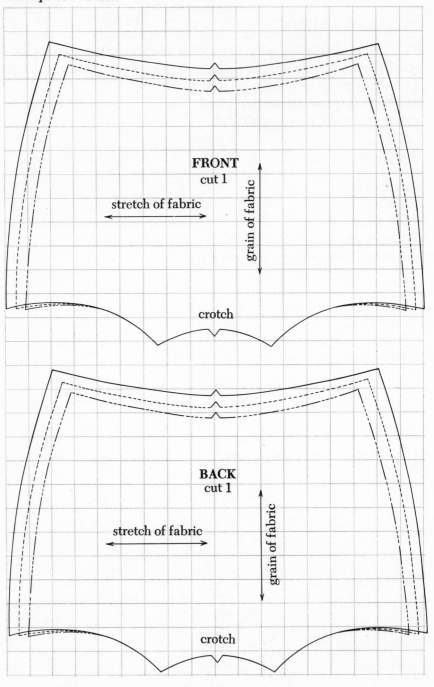

FRONT
cut 1

stretch of fabric

grain of fabric

crotch

BACK
cut 1

stretch of fabric

grain of fabric

crotch

......small
----medium
____large

2. Lay the fabric out flat and place the pattern pieces on it so that the stretch of the fabric will go *around* the body. Cut one each of the front and back pieces; cut two crotch pieces. If you are using tricot, you may wish to cut one of these from polyester-cotton single knit. This will serve as the crotch lining. Mark the right sides of all pieces with tape. If you wish to trim the panties with lace, do it now, following the instructions given on page 26.

3. Now join the front crotch seam. Place the front edge—the narrower side—of one crotch piece together with the front panty section, right sides together. Place the inner crotch piece—the cotton knit piece— in the same position but on the other side of the panty front so that its right side is against the wrong side of the panty. Pin it in place. You should now have three thicknesses of fabric at the seamline. Using a narrow zigzag with a short stitch length or a short straight stitch, join the seam (Diagram 1). Allow a ¼-inch seam and trim away the extra

Diagram 1

front

fabric close to the stitching. As you sew, stretch the crotch pieces and the panty front piece to fit.

4. To enclose the back crotch seam, place the panty front on the panty back, right sides together. Pin the right side of the outer crotch piece— the one now on the bottom—to the right side of the back panty piece (Diagram 2). Then bring the inner crotch piece around the top of

Diagram 2

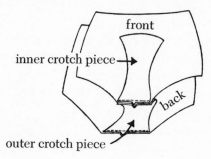

front

inner crotch piece

back

outer crotch piece

both panty pieces to the wrong side of the panty back; pin in place at the crotch seam. The right side of the inner crotch piece should now be against the wrong side of the back panty piece and both panty pieces will be rolled horizontally between the crotch pieces, as shown in Diagram 3. Once again, you should have three fabric thicknesses

Diagram 3

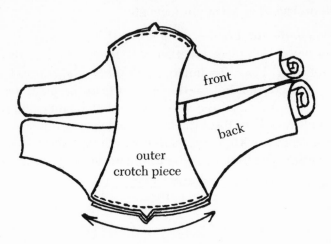

at the seamline. Join the seam as described in step 3, trim away the excess fabric, and pull the panty pieces out from between the crotch pieces; remove the tape markers from the crotch sections.

5. To join the side seams, place the front and back panty pieces right sides together. Widen the zigzag but keep the short stitch length for a rolled seam—or use a short straight stitch—and sew both seams; remove the remaining tape.

6. Determine the amount of waistband elastic you'll need by subtracting 4 inches from your waist measurement. Cut the elastic to this length and overlap the ends slightly; whip them together by hand or by machine zigzagging. Starting with the seam, divide the elastic into quarters, marking the divisions with pins. Then match the side seams of the panties to find the center front and center back (Diagram 4); mark these with pins. Last, match these two points to find the center of the sides; mark with pins. (The side seams will not be the centers of the sides because the back panty is larger than the front.)

Diagram 4

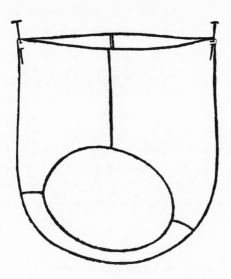

With the ruffled edge up, place the seam in the elastic against the wrong side of the center back of the panty; pin. Continue adding the elastic by matching pins to the pins on the panty top. If you want to cover the seam in the elastic so that it won't rub your skin, cut a 1½-inch square of fabric, fold it into thirds so that the raw edges overlap slightly, and run a line of short straight stitching down the center (Diagram 5). With the overlap facing the elastic, place the tab piece

Diagram 5

between the elastic and the panty, making sure that the top edges are even (Diagram 6). Using a narrow zigzag with a short stitch length or a short straight stitch, sew along the lower edge (the un-ruffled edge) of the elastic, starting at the center back and stretching the elastic to fit as you sew. Sew over the tab but not over the pins—

Diagram 6

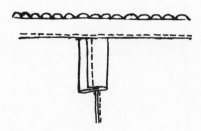

remove them before you get to them. Trim away the excess fabric under the elastic, being careful not to cut the tab, and turn the elastic to the outside of the panties. Turn the tab piece over the top edge of the elastic and tuck it under the bottom edge; stitch all around it in

Diagram 7

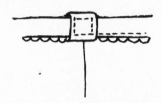

a rectangular pattern (Diagram 7). Continue stitching along the lower (ruffled) edge of the elastic.

7. Find the amount of elastic you'll need for each leg opening by subtracting about 2 inches from your thigh measurement. Cut two lengths of leg elastic to this measurement and join the ends as you did in step 6. Using the seam as one point, divide each in half and mark with a pin. With the ruffled edge down, place the seam of one elastic loop against the right side of one of the panty side seams. Place the midpoint of the elastic loop (marked with the pin) at the center of the crotch, and then move it about 1 inch toward the front of the panty to add fullness to the panty back. Beginning at either the front or the back of the crotch, stitch along the bottom edge of the elastic next to the ruffle, still using the narrow zigzag with a short stitch length or a short straight stitch. Stitch along the crotch first and then around the leg. As you sew, stretch the elastic to fit the panty except when you are stitching the crotch. When you've finished, the crotch should fit smoothly, without gathers. Trim any fabric that shows below the elastic. Repeat for the other leg.

Project 2

Hip Hugger Panties

The hip hugger panty differs from the panty brief only in that it is cut lower so that it rides down on the hips. This style is not only an essential one for low-slung pants and skirts but also one that will eliminate unnecessary bulk at the waistline, giving a freer line to body-clinging garments. It is also a more comfortable style for many women, especially those who find elastic at the waist restrictive and binding. Naturally, you can decorate these panties according to the mood of the moment, adding carnations and cardinals at will—try cutting them from printed fabrics and appliquéing them on—and using poppy-bright stretch laces instead of lingerie elastic. Incidentally, you can turn a panty brief pattern into a hip hugger pattern by simply cutting off the top 2½ inches from both the front and back pieces.

MATERIALS NEEDED:

½ yard nylon tricot *or* polyester-cotton single knit, 44 inches wide
small piece polyester-cotton single knit, for crotch lining (optional)
1 yard lingerie waist elastic, ½ inch wide, *or* stretch lace,
   ¾ to 1 inch wide
1½ yards lingerie leg elastic, ¼ inch wide, *or* stretch lace,
   ¾ to 1 inch wide
nylon lingerie *or* polyester thread

TOOLS NEEDED:

pattern paper
scissors
transparent tape
ballpoint pins
#9 ballpoint sewing-machine needle

PROCEDURE:

1. Since the hip hugger is basically a variation of the panty brief, follow the steps given in Project 1 (using the hip hugger pattern) unless you wish to use stretch lace instead of lingerie elastic. In that case, follow steps 1 through 5 of Project 1 and then steps 2 through 4 of this project.

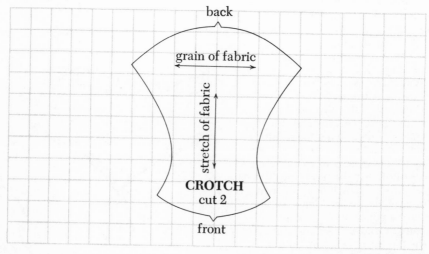

each square = 1 inch

each square = 1 inch

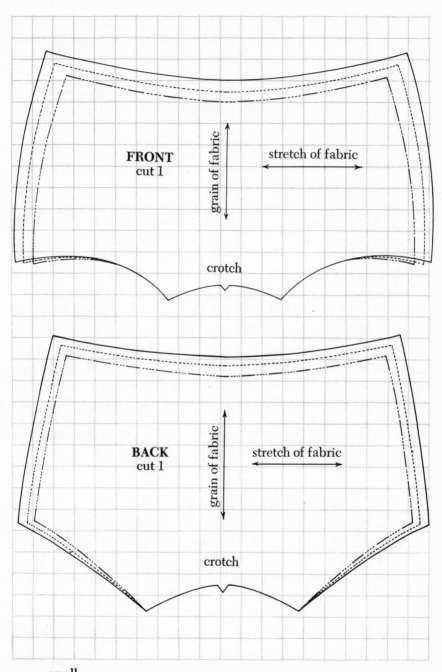

FRONT
cut 1

grain of fabric

stretch of fabric

crotch

BACK
cut 1

grain of fabric

stretch of fabric

crotch

39

2. To determine how much stretch lace you will need for the top opening, try on the hip huggers and stretch the lace snugly around the top edge of the panty. To find how much you will need for each leg opening, measure your thigh and subtract 2 to 4 inches from the result. Cut two pieces to this length. Overlap the ends of each piece and join them with a few hand whipstitches or machine zigzags.

3. To add the lace to the panty top, quarter the lace, starting with the seam and marking the divisions with pins. Then match the side seams of the panty to find the center front and back—mark these points with pins. Now match the center front and back to find the center of the sides; mark with pins. Place the seam in the lace at one of the panty side seams, wrong side of lace to right side of panty. With the top edge of the lace even with the top edge of the panty, match the pins in the lace to the pins in the panty. Using a narrow zigzag stitch with a short stitch length or a short straight stitch, sew along the bottom edge of the lace, stretching the lace to fit as you sew. Cut away the fabric from behind the lace close to the seamline.

4. To add the lace to the leg openings, fold both the lace loops and the leg openings in half, starting at the seams. Mark the divisions with pins. Place the wrong side of the lace against the right side of the panty with the seam in the lace at one panty side seam and the midpoint at the midpoint of the crotch. Move the midpoint of the lace about 1 inch toward the front of the crotch to add fullness to the panty back. The bottom edge of the lace should be even with the edge of the panty. Starting at either the front or the back of the crotch piece and using the same stitch that you did in step 3, sew along the top edge of the lace. Sew around the crotch piece first, being careful not to stretch the fabric so that the crotch will fit smoothly, without gathers. Continue stitching around the leg, stretching the lace to fit the panty as you sew. Trim away the fabric behind the lace close to the seamline. Repeat to add the elastic to the other leg opening.

Project 3
Bikini

The bikini, like the hip hugger, is similar to the panty brief. Since the only major difference is that the waistline is cut lower and the leg openings higher, construction is essentially the same if you are using lingerie elastic for the waist and leg openings. You may, however, prefer to use stretch lace in these spots. Most women find it more comfortable, and it gives a smoother line to outer wear. Available in nearly every color of the proverbial rainbow, it's also a lot prettier. To add your own touch, you might try it in a color that contrasts with the fabric—say, a moss green on a creamy tricot—and then you might cut out a few flower shapes from some extra lace and appliqué them to the panties. Or cut away the fabric from behind the appliqués, and let your skin shine through.

MATERIALS NEEDED:

½ yard nylon tricot *or* polyester-cotton single knit,
    44 inches wide
small piece polyester-cotton single knit, for crotch lining (optional)
1 yard lingerie waist elastic, ½ inch wide, *or* stretch lace,
    ¾ to 1 inch wide
1½ yards lingerie leg elastic, ¼ inch wide, *or* stretch lace,
    ¼ to ½ inch wide
nylon lingerie *or* polyester thread

TOOLS NEEDED:

pattern paper
scissors
transparent tape
ballpoint pins
#9 ballpoint sewing-machine needle

PROCEDURE:

1. Since the bikini is another variation of the panty brief in Project 1, you can put it together by following steps 1 through 5 of that project.

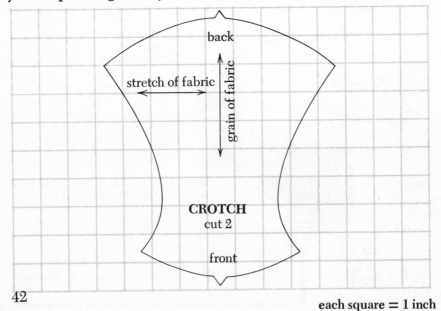

back

stretch of fabric

grain of fabric

CROTCH
cut 2

front

each square = 1 inch

Use the bikini pattern, and don't forget to lay out the pattern pieces on the fabric so that the stretch of the fabric will go around the body.

2. If you are using lingerie elastic at the top and leg openings, apply it by following steps 6 and 7 of Project 1. If you are using stretch lace instead, steps 2 through 4 of Project 2 will explain how to apply it.

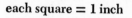

each square = 1 inch

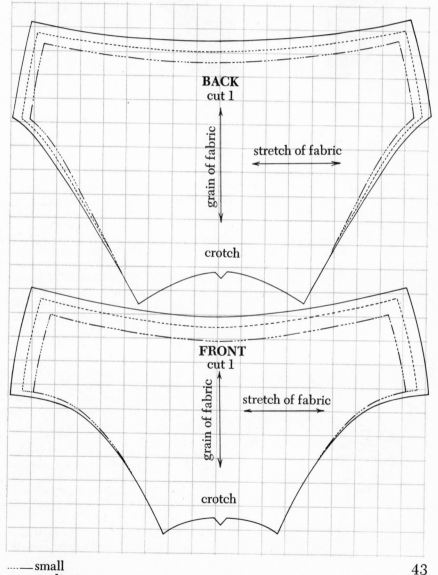

BACK
cut 1

grain of fabric

stretch of fabric

crotch

FRONT
cut 1

grain of fabric

stretch of fabric

crotch

·······— small
------- medium
_____ large

Project 4

French Bikini

Until very recent times, the French bikini was "it." No barer could one be, it was thought, but barer we are—with the advent of the string bikini. However, the string bikini is pretty much reserved for those who have very little to cover in the first place, which, unfortunately, leaves out a great many of us. For us, French is better—not to mention more comfortable. Compare the two styles and you'll see what we mean. And certainly the French version is more feminine, with its lace sides and soft body fabrics. Although we've called for the traditional undies fabrics for reasons of cost and practicality, you could make this bikini of something that's really lovely on the skin, something like Qiana or real silk or even panné velvet. It takes so little fabric and effort to make that you simply can't lose by experimenting.

MATERIALS NEEDED:

⅓ yard nylon tricot *or* polyester-cotton single knit, 32 inches wide
1½ yards stretch lace, ¼ to ½ inch wide
1 yard stretch lace, ¾ to 1 inch wide
nylon lingerie *or* polyester thread

TOOLS NEEDED:

pattern paper
scissors
transparent tape
ballpoint pins
#9 ballpoint sewing-machine needle

PROCEDURE:

1. Preshrink the bikini fabric. Then measure your hips to determine
your size according to the chart below.

small	*medium*	*large*
34–36 inches	36–38 inches	38–40 inches

On the pattern paper, enlarge both pattern pieces to size (page 17),
transfer any pattern markings, cut out the pieces, and label them.

each square = 1 inch

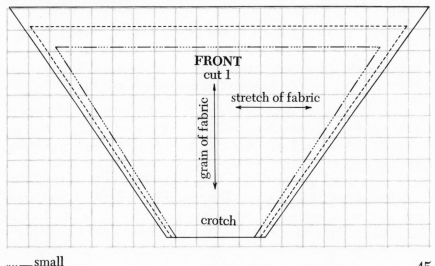

FRONT
cut 1

stretch of fabric

grain of fabric

crotch

.....— small
----- medium
——large

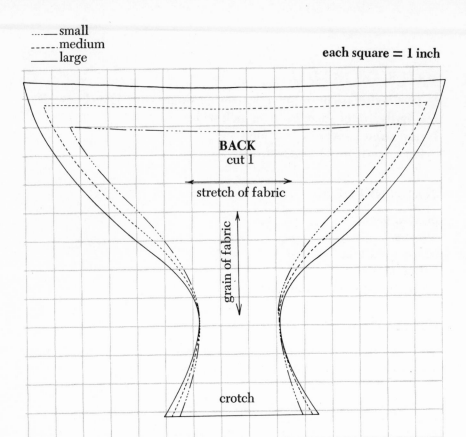

BACK
cut 1

stretch of fabric

grain of fabric

crotch

2. Lay the fabric out flat and place the pattern pieces on top, making certain that you follow the grain and stretch lines marked on the patterns. Cut one of each and mark their right sides with tape.

3. Using a narrow zigzag with a short stitch length or a short straight stitch, join the panty front to the back at the crotch seam. Make sure that the right sides are together and that you allow a ¼-inch seam allowance. Trim away the excess fabric close to the seamline.

4. Cut two pieces of narrow stretch lace—for the leg openings—to one of the following lengths: for a small, 17 inches; medium, 21 inches; or large, 25 inches. Find the middle of the lace pieces and mark with pins—do not sew together the ends as you have in earlier panty projects. Then match the top edges of the panty to find the center of the leg openings; mark with pins. With the panty laid out flat and right side up, pin one end of one lace piece, also right side up, to the top front edge and the other end to the top back edge, matching the mid-

dle of the lace to the middle of the panty leg opening (Diagram 1). Make sure that the edge of the lace is even with the edge of the panty fabric; then pin the lace in place. Sew along the inside edge of the lace, using a narrow zigzag with a short stitch length or a short

Diagram 1

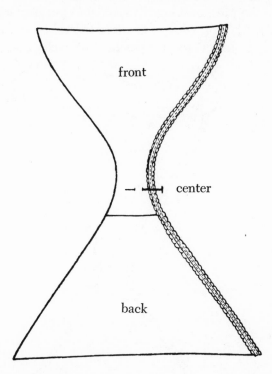

front

center

back

straight stitch, stretching the lace to fit the panty. Trim away the fabric that is behind the lace, cutting close to the seamline. Repeat this step to add the lace to the other leg opening.

5. Cut one piece of wide stretch lace for the top opening to one of the following lengths: for a small, 23½ inches; medium, 25½ inches; or large, 27½ inches. Overlap the ends slightly and sew them together with a zigzag stitch or a hand whipstitch. Starting at the seam, measure off 3 inches and mark with a pin—this section is for the right side of the panty. Then measure off 7 inches for a small size, 8 inches for a medium, or 9 for a large and mark with another pin—this section is for the top edge of the panty front. Measure off another 3 inches for the left-side section and mark it with a pin. The remaining section—

for the top edge of the panty back—should measure 10½ inches for a small size, 11½ for a medium, and 12½ for a large.

6. Lay the lace section for the panty front along the top edge of the fabric—the panty should be right side up and the lace should be right side up. Use the pins marking the section to pin the lace to each side (Diagram 2). The top edge of the lace should be even with the top edge of the panty. Place the section of lace designated for the

Diagram 2

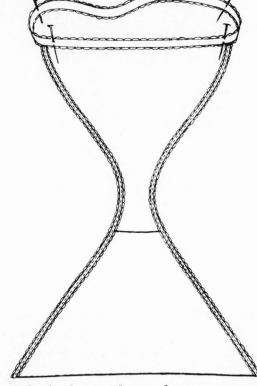

panty back along the back top edge in the same way and pin it in place. This will leave open the 3-inch sections on each side—there should be no fabric behind the lace. Still using the narrow zigzag with short stitch length or the short straight stitch, sew along the lower edge of the lace, stretching it as necessary to fit the panty. Continue sewing through the side sections of the lace, even though there is no fabric behind them. Trim the fabric away that is behind the stretch lace, cutting it close to the seamline.

Project 5

String Bikini

Here it is—the briefest of all bikinis.
To make it, we used a two-way stretch
fabric— 100-percent nylon single knit—
that is usually used for swimwear linings
and body suits. If you can find it only in
white, dye it or tie-dye it with household
dyes. If you find that this one-size-fits-all
pattern is too skimpy for you, you can
easily enlarge it. To lengthen it, add
equal amounts of fabric to the front
and back. To widen it, add equal
amounts to each side of the front and
back, tapering them to the crotch—the
crotch need not be widened. If you
have lengthened it, increase the leg
elastic by half the amount you added;
if you have widened it, increase the
front and back elastic by half the
amount you widened it.

MATERIALS NEEDED:

½ yard 100-percent nylon single knit with two-way stretch,
 12 inches wide
2 yards lingerie waist elastic, ½ inch wide
2 Luxite bone rings, ⅝ inch in diameter
nylon lingerie *or* polyester thread

TOOLS NEEDED:

pattern paper
scissors
ballpoint pins
#9 ballpoint sewing-machine needle

PROCEDURE:

1. Wash the fabric to preshrink it. Then enlarge the pattern on the pattern paper (page 17), making any adjustments you wish. Transfer any pattern markings, cut out the piece, and label it.

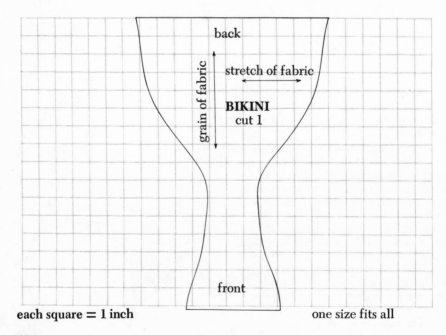

grain of fabric

back

stretch of fabric

BIKINI
cut 1

front

each square = 1 inch   one size fits all

50

2. Lay the pattern on the fabric, making sure to follow the grain and stretch lines marked on the pattern; cut out.

3. Cut the lingerie elastic into two 19-inch lengths for the legs and sides of the panties, one 9-inch length for the panty back, and one 5-inch length for the panty front.

4. Place the 5-inch length of elastic, ruffled edge up, on the wrong side of the panty front top edge—the narrower edge (Diagram 1).

Diagram 1

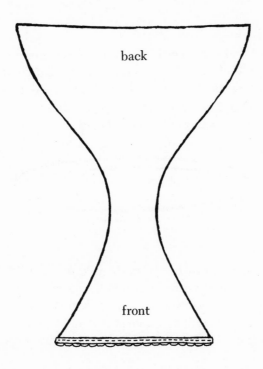

back

front

The elastic should overlap the panty top by about ¼ inch. Using a narrow zigzag with a short stitch length or a short straight stitch, sew along the bottom straight edge, stretching the elastic to fit the panty. Trim the fabric close to the seamline. Turn the elastic to the right side of the panty and stitch along the bottom edge—the ruffled edge. Add the 9-inch length of elastic to the top edge of the panty back in the same way.

51

5. Attach the bone rings to the 19-inch lengths of elastic: Using just 1 inch of elastic, thread one end of one piece of elastic through one ring. Using a narrow zigzag with a short stitch length or a short straight stitch, sew through both thicknesses of elastic, stitching across the width (Diagram 2). With the needle still in the elastic,

Diagram 2

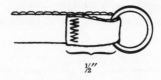

½″

turn the elastic and sew over it again to hold it firmly in place. Then thread the other end through the same ring and attach it to the opposite side, following the procedure above. You should now have a circle of elastic held together by a bone ring (Diagram 3). Repeat to add the other ring to the other length of elastic.

Diagram 3

6. Next, measure off 3½ inches from the fold of the elastic around the ring and mark the spot with a pin. Do the same on the other piece, but measure in the opposite direction. When the elastic is attached to the panty, the rings will be on each side of the top front edge and the sides of the panty will be the space between the rings and the pins (Diagram 4).

Diagram 4

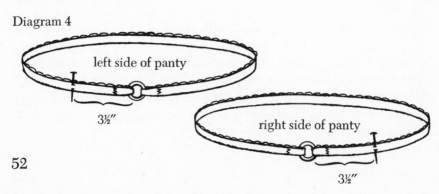

left side of panty

3½″

right side of panty

3½″

7. To attach the 19-inch lengths of elastic to the panty, place the pin marker in one elastic loop at one side of the top edge of the bikini back (Diagram 5). The elastic should be placed on the right side of

Diagram 5

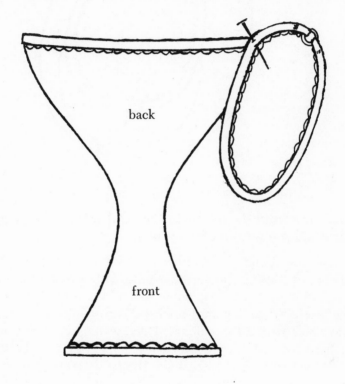

the panty and its ruffled edge should be pointing down. Pin the elastic to the fabric at this point. Repeat this procedure to add the other elastic loop to the other side.

8. Now pin each ring to one side of the top edge of the bikini front. Then bring together the front and back top edges of the bikini; with pins, mark the midpoints of the elastic loops and the panty leg openings. On each side, place the midpoint of the elastic at the midpoint of the panty leg opening and pin together (Diagram 6). Remember

Diagram 6

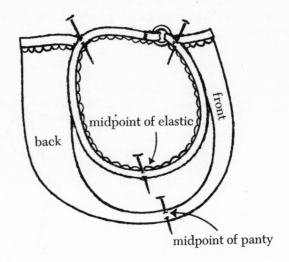

midpoint of panty

that the elastic should be on the right side of the panty with the ruffled edge toward the leg opening.

9. Starting at one end of either the front or the back top edge, begin sewing, still using the narrow zigzag with a short stitch length or a short straight stitch. Remember to hold the threads back away from the needle when you start sewing. With the threads held out of the way, backstitch a few stitches. Then, sewing along the straight edge of the elastic, stitch around each leg opening, stretching the elastic to fit the panty. Backstitch a few stitches to secure the elastic firmly, and then trim the fabric close to the seamlines. Your finished panty should have the bone ring on each side of the front of the panty.

Project 6

Pettipants

Whether you put the pettipant style of undies under a pair of lean French jeans or perfectly tailored flannel slacks, you will look better than ever, for that unsightly panty leg elastic line that has marred many a rear view will have disappeared completely. Pettipants are equally great with skirts because they not only eliminate the need for a slip but they also provide all the modesty you could ask for. And, they're a cinch to make—it's simply a matter of joining three pieces. If you feel creative, choose a pattern one size larger—to compensate for the lack of stretch in the fabric—and then make them out of silky white batiste, edge them with snowy white cotton lace, and team them up with a matching camisole. Or make them both up in a sheer voile or gauze for some cool-as-can-be summertime sleepwear.

MATERIALS NEEDED:

1 yard nylon tricot, 44 inches wide
1 yard lingerie waist elastic, ½ inch wide
1½ yards nylon lace, 1 to 2 inches wide
nylon lingerie *or* polyester thread

TOOLS NEEDED:

pattern paper
scissors
transparent tape
ballpoint pins
#9 ballpoint sewing-machine needle

PROCEDURE:

1. Preshrink the tricot before you begin. Then measure your hips to determine your size according to the chart below.

small	*medium*	*large*
34–36 inches	36–38 inches	38–40 inches

Enlarge both pattern pieces to size on the pattern paper (page 17), transfer any pattern markings, cut out the pieces, and label them.

2. Lay the tricot out flat and place the pattern pieces on it, making certain to follow the grain and stretch lines marked on the pattern. Cut one panty piece, flop the pattern, and cut another; cut two crotch pieces. Mark the right side of each main piece with a strip of tape placed at the center of the front edge; mark the right sides of the crotch pieces with two strips of tape placed on the two front edges. This will make finding the front edges easier while you are constructing the pettipants.

3. Place the two crotch pieces wrong sides together—you will work as though the two pieces were one, since you cannot enclose the crotch seams on pettipants. Place one front edge of the crotch piece between the two notches on the center front edge of one of the pettipant pieces, right sides together. Using a wide zigzag with a short stitch length, roll the seam between the notches. Begin and end the

each square = 1 inch

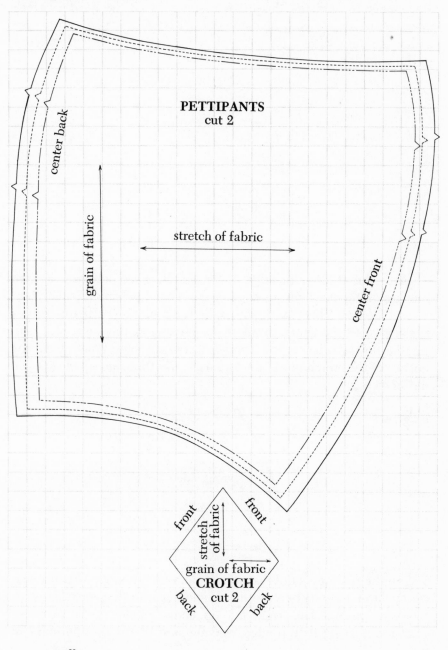

PETTIPANTS
cut 2

center back

grain of fabric

stretch of fabric

center front

front

stretch of fabric

grain of fabric

CROCH
cut 2

front

back

back

.... small
----- medium
—— large

stitching ¼ inch in from each end of the crotch piece (Diagram 1). Remember to hold the threads back away from the needle before you start to sew. If your machine doesn't have a zigzag feature, use a short straight stitch, sew a ¼-inch seam, and trim the fabric close to the seamline.

Diagram 1

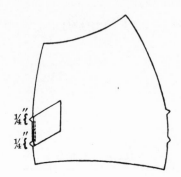

4. Place the other front edge of the crotch piece between the two notches on the center front edge of the second pettipant piece, right sides together. Then, with the right sides of the pettipant pieces together, join the center front seam, starting at the waist and continuing through the crotch piece. End the stitching ¼ inch from the bottom of the crotch piece (Diagram 2). Use the same stitch that you did in step 3.

Diagram 2

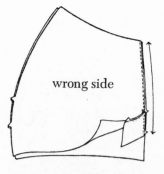

wrong side

5. Lay the pettipants out flat on a table, right side up. Measure one leg opening and cut two pieces of nylon lace to that measurement. Run each piece of lace, right side up, across one leg of the garment, and tape it along its top edge, making sure that its bottom edge is

even with the edge of the leg opening. Now, stitch along the top edge of the lace, using the wide zigzag stitch but with a medium stitch length (Diagram 3). You can also use a medium straight stitch. Trim away the fabric from behind the lace, cutting close to the stitching.

Diagram 3

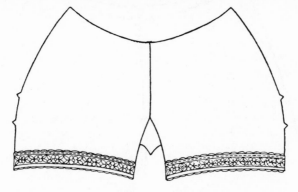

6. Fold one side of the pettipants in half, right sides together. Place one back edge of the crotch piece between the notches on the center back edge of the pettipant. Starting ¼ inch down from the top of the crotch piece, roll the crotch seam and the leg seam, using a wide zigzag with a short stitch length or a short straight stitch and trimming the seam close to the stitching (Diagram 4).

Diagram 4

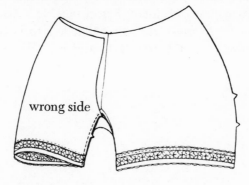

wrong side

7. Fold in half, right sides together, the other side of the pettipants, placing the remaining open edge of the crotch piece between the two notches. Starting at the waist, roll the center back seam, using the

59

same stitch that you did in step 6. Continue the stitching through the crotch piece to the bottom of the leg opening (Diagram 5).

Diagram 5

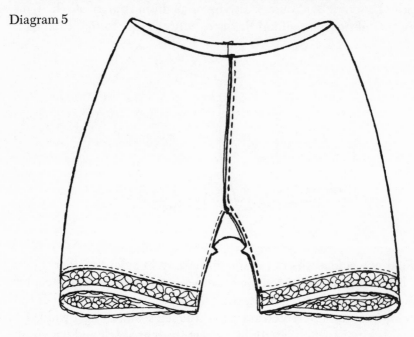

8. For the waist elastic, you will need a length that is 3 or 4 inches less than your waist measurement. Before cutting it, stretch the elastic around your waist to make sure that that length is comfortable for you. Then follow Project 1, step 6, to add it to the pettipants.

Project 7
Pants Liner

Now that slacks move freely from Saturday afternoon football games to formal church weddings, the pants liner has become the thing of today. In fact, no undie wardrobe is complete without a pair, even if they are reserved for just your latest Chinoise pantsuit, for certainly clothing that splendid deserves the unspoiled line that only a pants liner can give. Slacks that are light in color will receive double benefit, for the pants liner will intensify and smooth out that color. Incidentally, a well-fitting commercial slack pattern with an elastic waist can serve as a pants liner pattern—just trim the waist seam allowance to ½ inch and the others to ¼ inch. Straighten flared legs by drawing a line across the knee and then, from each end of that line, a line to the bottom of the leg; adjust the length to meet the ankle.

MATERIALS NEEDED:

1½ yards nylon tricot, 60 inches wide
1 yard lingerie waist elastic, ½ inch wide
1¾ yards nylon lace, 1 to 1½ inches wide,
    for bottom of legs (optional)
nylon lingerie *or* polyester thread

TOOLS NEEDED:

pattern paper
scissors
transparent tape
ballpoint pins
#9 ballpoint sewing-machine needle

PROCEDURE:

1. Before beginning, preshrink the tricot. Then take your hip measurement to determine your size according to the chart below.

small	*medium*	*large*
34–36 inches	36–38 inches	38–40 inches

Enlarge both pattern pieces to size on the pattern paper (page 17), transfer any pattern markings, cut out the pieces, and label them.

2. To make sure of a perfect, smooth fit, check your crotch measurement before cutting the fabric. Sitting on a hard, flat surface, such as a tabletop, tie a string around your waist—this will indicate your natural waistline—and measure from the side of your waistline to the point at which your thigh meets the tabletop. Add 1 inch to this figure. Then measure from the waist to the crotch line on the front pattern piece and compare the results. If you need to shorten the crotch, fold the pattern up on the line between the crotch and the waist (Diagram 1). If you need to lengthen it, cut the pattern apart on this line, place

Diagram 1

each square = 1 inch

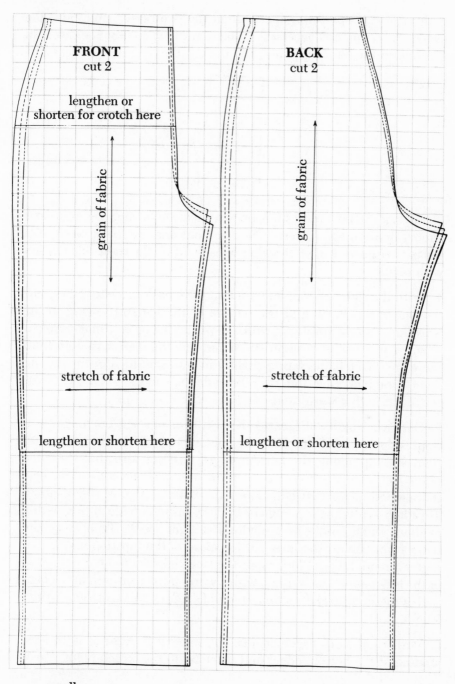

FRONT
cut 2

lengthen or
shorten for crotch here

grain of fabric

stretch of fabric

lengthen or shorten here

BACK
cut 2

grain of fabric

stretch of fabric

lengthen or shorten here

..... small
----- medium
____ large

63

a sheet of extra pattern paper behind the two pieces, and move the pieces as far apart as necessary (Diagram 2). Then tape the pieces in position to the backing paper, and cut out the lengthened pieces.

Diagram 2

3. Lay the pattern pieces out on the tricot, following the grain and stretch lines on the pattern. Cut one front and one back piece; flop the patterns over and cut another of each. Mark the right side of each with tape.

4. With the right sides of one front and one back piece together, sew the side seam, starting at the bottom of the leg and sewing to the waistline. Use a wide zigzag with a short stitch length to make a rolled seam, or use a short straight stitch and sew the seam ¼ inch in from the edge. Stretch the fabric slightly as you sew to prevent the leg seam from puckering. Join the other side seam in the same way. Press the seams with a warm iron.

5. Cut two lengths of lace to the width of one leg opening. With right sides up, lay the two leg pieces flat. Tape the lace, also right side up, along the bottom edges, making sure that the edge of the lace is even with the edge of the fabric. If one edge of the lace is scalloped, place that edge along the bottom edge of the opening. Topstitch across the top edge of the lace, using a wide zigzag with a medium stitch length or a medium straight stitch. Trim away the tricot from behind the lace, cutting close to the topstitching. If you prefer a more tailored look, omit the lace and turn the bottom edges of the legs under ¼ inch; press with a warm iron. Topstitch in the hem with a medium straight stitch or a wide zigzag and a medium stitch length.

6. With right sides together, join the inner leg seams of both legs, starting at the bottom edges and stitching to the crotch point. Use a

wide zigzag with a short stitch length to make a rolled seam or a short straight stitch with a ¼-inch seam allowance. Stretch the fabric slightly as you sew to prevent puckering. Topstitch the lace at the seams for added strength. Press the seams with a warm iron.

7. To join the crotch seam, one leg should be right side out and one, wrong side out. Place the right-side-out leg inside the other leg so that the right sides of both legs are together (Diagram 3). Stitch the

Diagram 3

crotch seam, using the rolled seam method or a short straight stitch with a ¼-inch seam allowance.

8. Apply the waist elastic as described in Project 1, step 6.

Project 8

Contour Bra, Padded or Not

Did you know that you can make four or five tricot bras for less than the price of one store-bought? That's exclusive of the trim, of course, and it's with the trim that you can really have the fun. You can inset lace panels, as we show in this project, stencil on some tiny fleur-de-lis in a deeper color, or turn each cup into a many-petaled flower with the embroiderer's satin stitch. Or you might make the upper cup pieces of lace and the lower of tricot—or vice versa. However you decide to use your imagination, the finished result will, we guarantee, fit better, wear longer, and be prettier than any bra you could buy at any price. A final bonus is that you can pad it or not, as you wish. You might try making one of each version, for one style will be better suited to certain wearing apparel than the other.

MATERIALS NEEDED:

¼ yard Lycra spandex, 22 inches wide
¼ yard nylon tricot, 48 inches wide
¼ yard fiberfill, 24 inches wide, for padding (optional)
¼ yard lace paneling, 24 inches wide, in color to match or contrast
    with other fabrics (optional)
approximately 2 yards lingerie plush elastic, ⅜ to ½ inch wide
1 bra-back closure, hook-and-eye type, commercially made
nylon lingerie *or* polyester thread

TOOLS NEEDED:

pattern paper
scissors
transparent tape
ballpoint pins
#9 ballpoint sewing-machine needle

PROCEDURE:

1. Before you begin, preshrink the tricot. Then enlarge the four pattern pieces to size on the pattern paper (page 17), using the same

each square = 1 inch

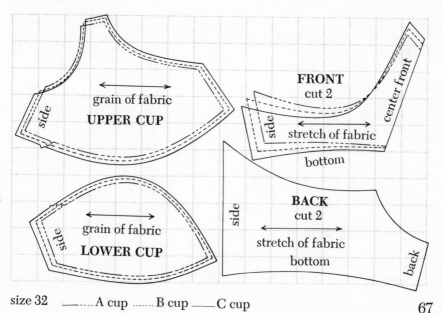

size 32 ——····· A cup ······· B cup ——C cup

each square = 1 inch

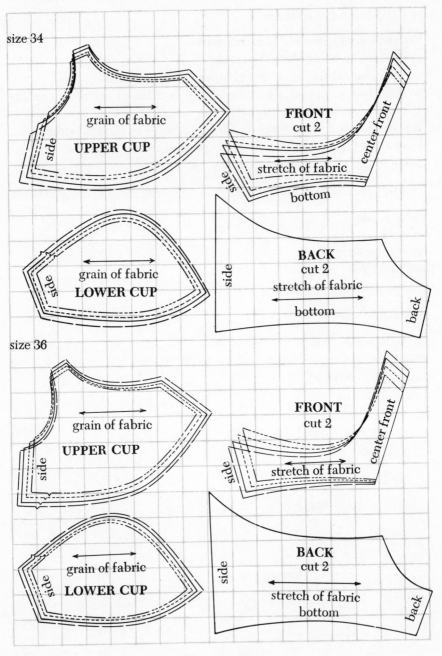

size 34

grain of fabric
UPPER CUP
side

FRONT
cut 2
center front
side
stretch of fabric
bottom

grain of fabric
LOWER CUP
side

BACK
cut 2
side
stretch of fabric
bottom
back

size 36

grain of fabric
UPPER CUP
side

FRONT
cut 2
center front
side
stretch of fabric

grain of fabric
LOWER CUP
side

BACK
cut 2
side
stretch of fabric
bottom
back

......A cup ......B cup ___C cup __ __D cup

size pattern that you would normally buy in a commercially manufactured bra. If you are planning to pad the bra, choose a cup size that is one size larger than you would normally wear. Transfer any pattern markings, cut out the pieces, and label them.

2. Lay the tricot out flat and place the piece for the upper cup and the piece for the lower cup on it. Make sure that you follow the grain lines marked on the pattern pieces when you lay them out. Cut two of each; then flop the patterns and cut two more of each, so that you have both a right and a left cup. If you are using lace paneling for the outer cups, cut only two upper and two lower cup pieces from the tricot, for lining. Then cut two upper and two lower cup pieces from the lace paneling. If you are going to pad the bra, cut two more of each piece from the fiberfill—don't forget to flop the patterns to cut the second pieces. From the Lycra, cut two center pieces and two back pieces, once again making certain to flop the patterns to cut the second pieces. Also, make sure that you have followed the pattern markings for the grain and stretch. If you wish to add extra support to the cups, cut two extra lower cup pieces from the Lycra and insert one between each two lower cup pieces when you are assembling the bra. Now mark the right side of each piece with a strip of transparent tape, and add whatever bits of lace or embroidery you wish while the bra is still flat. A word of caution before you begin constructing the bra: As you work, keep the cups lying out in front of you so that you don't end up with two right or two left cups—it can happen!

3. If you are padding the bra, place each fiberfill cup piece against the wrong side of a corresponding fabric cup piece—you should have four cup pieces left over, which will become the bra lining. If you are adding extra support to the bra, place each Lycra cup piece against a corresponding fabric cup piece, right side to wrong side. Now join the upper cup pieces to the lower cup pieces: With the right sides together, join one upper cup piece to one lower cup piece at the center seam, allowing a ¼-inch seam allowance and using either a narrow zigzag stitch with a short stitch length or a short straight stitch (Diagram 1). Repeat to construct the other cup, making sure that you have both a right and a left cup. If you have padded the bra, you will have four thicknesses at the seamline; if you have added Lycra for extra support, you will have three thicknesses; if you have

done both, you will have five. Now join the remaining upper and lower cup pieces in the same way—these will become the lining.

Diagram 1

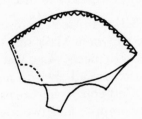

4. Place the lining pieces against the outer bra pieces, wrong sides together, to check for proper fit. Adjust if necessary. Then with a wide zigzag and medium stitch length, topstitch the center seams on all four cup pieces (Diagram 2). If you don't have a zigzag machine, use

Diagram 2

a short straight stitch on each side of the seam (Diagram 3). Since you will be topstitching all the seams on the bra to achieve smooth

Diagram 3

lines, you will have to remember constantly to change the width of the zigzag and the length of the stitch.

70

5. Replace the liners inside the cups, wrong sides together; pin if you wish. Then, with the right sides together, match the curved edge of one center cup piece to the lower edge of the main cup piece and stitch through all three thicknesses, using either a narrow zigzag with a short stitch length or a short straight stitch. Allow a ¼-inch seam allowance. Repeat for the other cup. Then turn the bra cups over and topstitch each seam, pushing the seam allowances toward the Lycra as you sew to prevent the Lycra from scratching your skin (Diagram 4). Don't forget to change the width and length of your stitch before topstitching.

Diagram 4

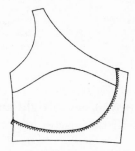

6. With right sides together, join a back piece to the side of each bra cup, allowing ¼-inch seams. Topstitch, pushing the seams to the back, toward the Lycra (Diagram 5).

Diagram 5

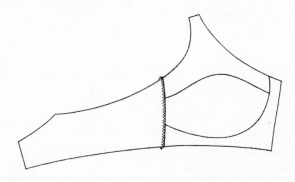

7. Right sides together, place the back edge of one strap against one back piece—the strap will temporarily dangle. The proper placement

71

for the strap is the point just before the back begins to curve toward the back closing (Diagram 6). Using a small straight stitch, sew the strap to the bra about ¼ inch in from the edge. Repeat to add the other strap.

Diagram 6

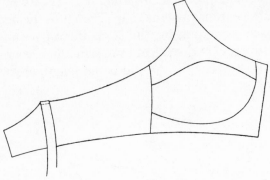

8. Your bra is still in two pieces—a right and a left side. Before you join them, you must add the elastic to the top edge (Diagram 7).

Diagram 7

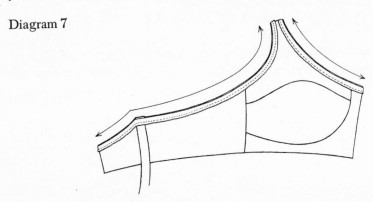

With the picot edge down and the plush side up, place the elastic on the right side of the bra, starting it at the center front and making sure that the top edge of the elastic is even with the top edge of the fabric. Using a narrow zigzag with a short stitch length or a short straight stitch, sew the bottom edge, right next to the picot trim, to the bra. Start at the center front and stitch to the point at which the front of the strap will be attached. Cut the elastic at that point. Replace the elastic on the other side of the strap and continue stitching it to the bra all the way to the back edge. When you reach the back-strap attachment point, ease the elastic around it, being careful not to stretch it. Then cut away the Lycra from behind the elastic along the back top edge. Finally, turn the elastic to the wrong side of the bra and topstitch it in place, ¼ inch in from the edge.

9. Join the bra halves by placing them right sides together and stitching down the center seam, using a short straight stitch. Open the seam and topstitch down the center with a zigzag stitch or down each side with a straight stitch (Diagram 8). If this center seam irritates

Diagram 8

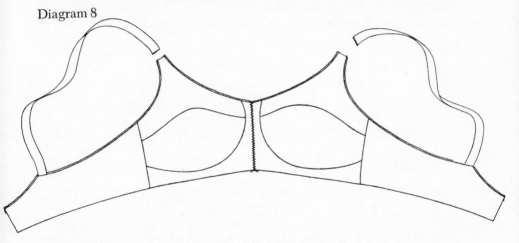

your skin, a tricot facing may be added before the seam is topstitched: Cut a strip of tricot the same length as the center seam and ½ inch wide. Place the strip over the opened seam on the wrong side of the bra and then topstitch. The topstitching will hold the facing in place.

10. To add the elastic to the bottom edge of the bra, place it, plush side up and picot edge up, against the right side of the bra. Stitch right next to the picot trim, turn the elastic under to the wrong side of the bra, and topstitch it ¼ inch in from the bottom edge.

11. Remove the elastic from the eye portion of the bra closure, and insert the left side of the bra back piece between the two pieces of fabric; join them by stitching in a rectangular shape (Diagram 9).

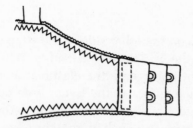

Diagram 9

Use a short straight stitch and be careful to avoid the metal eyes as you sew. To add the hook section, fold it in half so that the wrong sides are together and insert the right side of the bra back piece between the folds, making sure that the hooks are on the wrong side of the bra. Using a zipper foot and sewing on the wrong side of the bra, stitch as close to the hooks as possible. Then stitch from each end of that seam to the edge of the bra back (Diagram 10).

Diagram 10

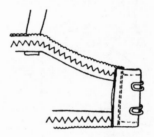

12. To attach the shoulder straps to the front of the bra, turn the top edges of the bra strap extensions under ½ inch and place them on top of the front ends of the straps. Join them by sewing with a short straight stitch in a triangular pattern. If your machine won't sew through that many thicknesses, try placing the strap on top of the bra and then sewing it in a triangle. If the straps you're using are made of two pieces of tricot, you can place the bra edge between the two strap pieces and then sew the three pieces together.

Project 9
Convertible Body Bra

This barely-there essence of a bra is a one-size-fits-all design and one that is exceptionally easy to make. Just one pattern piece is all there is to it. Although we've used a two-way stretch nylon, we've seen this style happily done in white organdy, embroidered with tiny red hearts, and combined with a heart-embroidered French bikini. To make a sensational swimsuit, try a boldly striped polyester-cotton knit and team it up with a string bikini. Because so little fabric is required, rummage through your fabric scrap bag before you skip out to the fabric store—you may have just the thing. Almost anything light enough in weight to hug the body curves will do. An added feature of this bra is that it can be worn under nearly any style of dress, for the straps can be worn crisscrossed, halter-style, or straight.

MATERIALS NEEDED:

¼ yard two-way stretch fabric, 86- to 87-percent nylon and 13- to 14-percent Lycra spandex, 15 inches wide

1 yard lingerie leg elastic, ¼ inch wide

1 yard lingerie plush elastic, ¾ inch wide

1¼ yards lingerie plush elastic, ½ inch wide

1 yard stretch lace, ¾ inch wide

1 bra hook closure, 1 inch wide, or hook-and-eye closure, commercially made

2 adjustable shoulder strap slides, ½-inch size, and 4 bra hook closures, ½ inch size, or 4 combination bra hook closures and adjustable strap slides from old bra with detachable straps (see step 8)

nylon lingerie or polyester thread

TOOLS NEEDED:

pattern paper

scissors

transparent tape

ballpoint pins

#9 ballpoint sewing-machine needle

PROCEDURE:

1. Enlarge the pattern piece to size on the pattern paper (page 17), transfer any pattern markings, cut out the piece, and label it.

2. Lay the pattern on the fabric, making sure that the grain line on the pattern is on the grain of the fabric. Cut out, flop the pattern over, and cut a second piece. You should have both a right and a left cup.

3. Gather the lower edge of the cup from the center front to the notch. To do this, stitch ¼ inch in from the edge with a medium-length straight stitch. Pulling on the threads, gather the fabric enough to measure 4½ inches from the center front to the notch. Repeat for the other cup.

4. Cut two pieces of ¼-inch-wide lingerie leg elastic to 4½ inches long and two pieces to 5 inches long. Place the 4½-inch lengths along the

each square = 1 inch

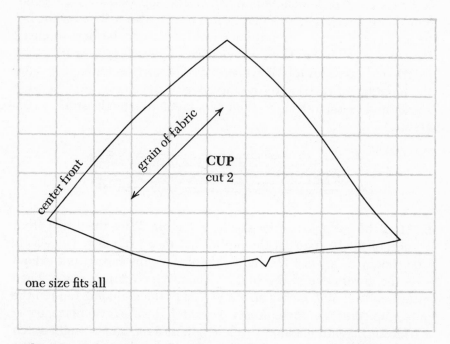

grain of fabric

center front

CUP
cut 2

one size fits all

right side of the center front edges of the bra; place the 5-inch lengths along the outer edges of the bra cups (Diagram 1). Stitch in place, stretching the elastic to fit the cups and using a narrow zigzag with a short stitch length or a short straight stitch.

Diagram 1

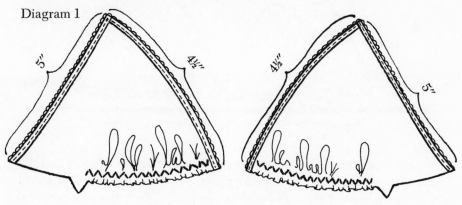

5. Cut a piece of ¾-inch-wide plush elastic approximately 25 inches long. With 2 inches of one end turned under—this will be for the bra hook—run the elastic around your ribs just under the bust to check for a comfortable fit. Then cut a piece of stretch lace to the same length and lay it on top of the smooth side of the elastic. Topstitch the top edge of the lace to the top edge of the elastic, using a wide zigzag and medium-length stitch or a medium straight stitch (Diagram 2).

Diagram 2

6. Mark the midpoint of the elastic with a pin. Place the center front corners of the bra cups at the pin so that they just meet. The elastic side should be against the right side of the cups and should extend over the lower edge of the cups by about ¼ inch. Pin in place. Then measure off about 6 inches on either side of the midpoint and pin the outer cup corners at these points. Topstitch the elastic in place, using a wide zigzag and medium stitch length or a medium straight stitch and stretching the elastic to fit the cups (Diagram 3).

Diagram 3

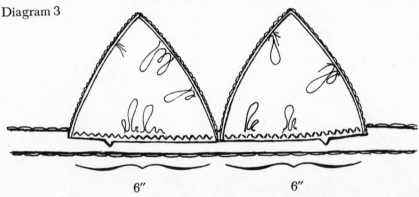

6"   6"

7. Cut four pieces of ½-inch-wide plush elastic to 1¼ inches long. Fold the pieces in half, plush sides together, and topstitch one of these to the wrong side of the top point of each cup. Place the other two on the wrong side of the elastic about 2 inches from the outside corner of each bra cup (Diagram 4). Topstitch in place, using a wide zigzag

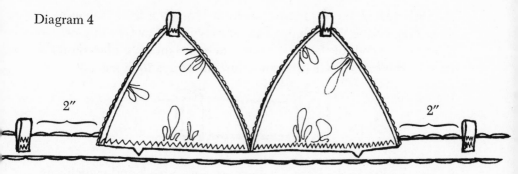

Diagram 4

2″   2″

and medium stitch length or a medium straight stitch. These form the loops for the strap hooks.

8. To make the straps, cut two pieces of ½-inch-wide plush elastic to a length of 18 inches. The straps will need some type of hook and adjustable slide so that the straps may be changed from straight to halter to crisscross. Old store-bought strapless bras with detachable straps will usually have what you need—a combination hook and adjuster. These are difficult to buy in the stores yet. If you have them available, thread each end of the two pieces of elastic through the four hook and slide adjusters in the same way as the original straps were (Diagram 5). If you don't have any, buy two ½-inch adjustable

Diagram 5

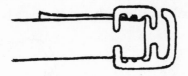

shoulder strap slides and four ½-inch bra hook closures, or use the strap slides from an old bra and just buy the bra hook closures. (The bra hook closure is the same type used to close the bra back but in a smaller size.) Place two bra hook closures on one end of each piece of elastic by threading the elastic through the top of the hook. The plush side of the elastic should be next to the skin. Using a zipper foot, stitch the elastic close to the hook with a short straight stitch. On the other end of each piece of elastic, thread the elastic through the strap slide, then through the top of the hook, and back up through the slide (Diagram 6). It isn't necessary to stitch this. It's easier to thread the elastic through the slide when you use another bra strap as a guide. The ends of the elastic with the slides on it are placed on the front of the bra so that you can adjust the straps to fit easily.

Diagram 6

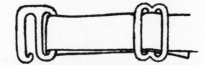

9. For the bra-back closure, you can sew on a hook-and-eye closing, following the instructions given in step 11 of Project 8, or you can use a bra slide closure. For the latter, place the hook on the right-hand elastic edge and thread 1 inch of the elastic through it, turning it under (Diagram 7). With a zipper foot and a short straight stitch,

Diagram 7

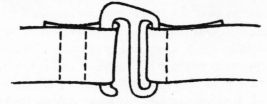

stitch close to the hook and again at the edge of the elastic that was turned under. Stitch the left-hand edge of the back elastic in the same way, leaving an opening through which to insert the hook. The finished bra should look like that shown in Diagram 8.

Diagram 8

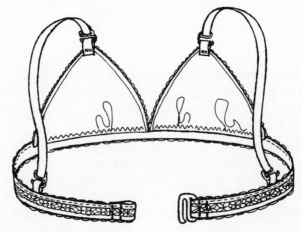

Project 10
Leisure Bra

This comfy little body shaper, also known as a sleepwear bra and a sport bra, has no back opening—no hooks and eyes to dig into a sublimely relaxed body. Of course, no back opening means that it must be pulled over the head to get it on, so we've made it in a two-way stretch fabric. You will probably find this fabric with the swimwear or body-suit fabrics rather than with the lingerie. Two pattern pieces are all that are necessary for this one-size-fits-all natural-look style. All the seams should be sewn with a ¼-inch seam allowance and all the stitching should be done with a short stitch length. (If you have a zigzag feature on your machine, set it for narrow.)

MATERIALS NEEDED:

⅝ yard two-way stretch fabric, either cotton knit with Lycra spandex
  or 100-percent nylon, 18 inches wide
2¼ yards stretch lace, ⅜ to ½ inch wide
¾ yard stretch lace, 1 inch wide
nylon lingerie *or* polyester thread

TOOLS NEEDED:

pattern paper
scissors
ballpoint pins
#9 ballpoint sewing-machine needle

PROCEDURE:

1. Enlarge the pattern pieces to size on the pattern paper (page 17),
transfer any pattern markings, cut out the pieces, and label them.

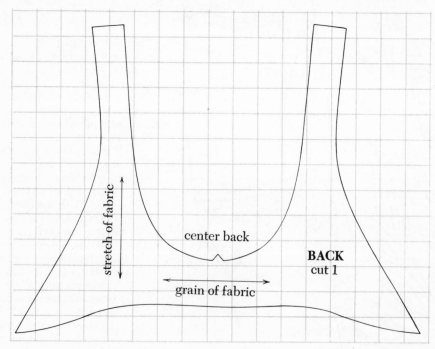

stretch of fabric

center back

grain of fabric

BACK
cut 1

each square = 1 inch
one size fits all

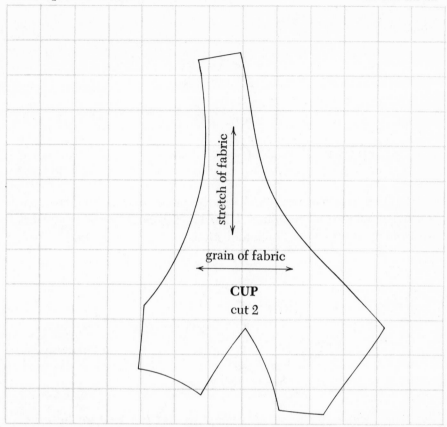

2. Lay the pattern pieces out on the fabric so that the grain of the fabric will go around the body. You will need to cut one back piece and two cup pieces—a right and a left. If you are cutting one cup at a time, be sure to turn over the pattern before cutting the fabric so that you will have both a right and a left cup.

3. Stitch the darts in the front cups, and then, with right sides together, join the shoulder seams; trim the shoulder seams close to the stitching.

4. Cut two 20-inch lengths of the narrower stretch lace to edge the armholes. Place one length of the lace, right side up, around the outside of one armhole. Beginning at the back of the armhole, stitch along the inside edge of the lace, stretching the lace slightly to fit (Diagram 1). Make sure that the outer edge of the lace is even

Diagram 1

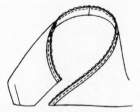

with the edge of the armhole. Trim the fabric from behind the lace, cutting close to the seamline. Then lap the back piece of the bra over the front by about ¼ inch and stitch in place (Diagram 2). Trim

Diagram 2

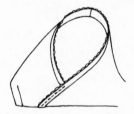

the fabric close to the seam. Repeat to add the lace to the other armhole.

5. Cut one 36-inch length of narrow stretch lace to edge the front, shoulder, and back neckline. With the midpoint of the lace at the notch on the center back, bring the ends of the lace up over the shoulders and around to the center front (Diagram 3). The top edge

Diagram 3

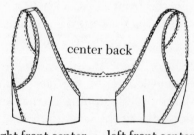

center back

right front center   left front center

of the lace should be even with the edge of the fabric. Starting at the center front edge of the left cup and stretching the lace slightly to fit, stitch along the inner edge of the lace. You will finish at the center front of the right cup. Trim away the fabric from behind the lace, close to the seamline.

6. Cut one 23½-inch length of the 1-inch-wide stretch lace and place it along the bottom edge of the bra, wrong side against right side. The top edge of the lace should overlap the bottom edge of the bra by about ¼ inch, which means that the lower ¾ inch of lace will have no fabric behind it (Diagram 4). Pin the midpoint of the lace at the

Diagram 4

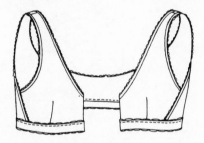

center back notch of the bra; also pin the lace to the right and left center front of the bra. Topstitch along the top edge of the lace, stretching it slightly as you sew.

7. Join the center seam, right sides together. Trim away the excess fabric, cutting as close as possible to the stitching.

Project 11
Convertible Bandeau Bra

This little bit of a bra spanning the body to fit whatever there is to fit represents perhaps the ultimate in the no-bra look. Essentially, nothing more than a band—hence, its French name *bandeau*—it offers the bare minimum in curvature control. With only one pattern piece, this one-size-fits-all design requires a minimum of effort to put together, too; however, construction should be done with a zigzag stitch in order for the bra to have that all-important stretch-ability. If you don't have a zigzag machine, try straight stitching while you are stretching the fabric as much as possible. Within about half an hour, it should be ready to wear and in any one of four ways—strapless, halter-style, crisscross-style, or straight. If you'd like an opaque bra to wear under see-through garb, try recycling a body suit or leg tights for the fabric.

MATERIALS NEEDED:

¾ yard stretch tricot *or* 100-percent nylon single knit
    with two-way stretch, 28 inches wide
2½ yards lingerie plush elastic, ⅜ to ½ inch wide
6 inches grosgrain ribbon, ⅜ inch wide, in color of your choice
2 adjustable shoulder strap slides, ½ inch size, and 4 bra
    hook closures, ½ inch size, *or* 4 combination bra hook closures and
    adjustable strap slides from old bra with detachable straps
nylon lingerie *or* polyester thread

TOOLS NEEDED:

pattern paper
scissors
transparent tape
ballpoint pins
#9 ballpoint sewing-machine needle

PROCEDURE:

1. Enlarge the pattern piece on the pattern paper (page 17), transfer
any pattern markings, cut it out, and label it.

each square = 1 inch

top

BRA
cut 1

place on fold

center front

greatest amount of stretch

back seam

dart

bottom

·····— size 32   ····· size 34   —— size 36

2. Lay the pattern piece on the fabric so that the stretch of the fabric goes around the body. Cut out and mark the right side with tape.

3. Using a wide zigzag with a short stitch length (or a short straight stitch with a ¼-inch seam allowance), sew the front darts, making a rolled seam. Stitch from the bottom of the dart to the point; then, with the needle still in the fabric, turn the fabric and stitch back a few stitches to lock them in place.

4. With the plush side up and the straight edge at the edge of the bra top, place the elastic along the right side of the top edge of the bra. Stitch close to the picot edge of the elastic, using a narrow zigzag with a short stitch length or a short straight stitch (Diagram 1).

Diagram 1

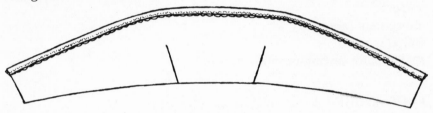

5. Turn the elastic to the wrong side of the bra so that the picot trim points up. Topstitch it on the right side of the bra, using a wide zigzag and medium-length stitch or a medium straight stitch. Cut the elastic at the edge. Add the elastic along the bottom edge of the bra in the same way as described above.

6. With the right sides together, stitch the back seam in the bra, sewing through both the top and the bottom elastic. Use a wide zigzag with a short stitch length to make a rolled seam or a short straight stitch with a ¼-inch seam allowance (Diagram 2). Then turn the bra

Diagram 2

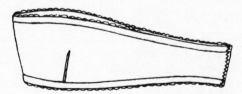

right side out and topstitch down the middle of the seam, using a wide zigzag and a medium-length stitch or a medium straight stitch on each side of the seam. Again, sew through the top and the bottom elastic to lock the stitching and give added strength to the seam.

7. Cut four pieces of ribbon 1 inch long; fold each in half. Place one on each side of the back seam about 2 inches from the seam and on the wrong side of the bra (Diagram 3). The folded edges should

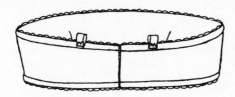

extend slightly above the top of the elastic in order to provide loops for the strap hooks. Attach them to the bra by zigzagging over the topstitching two or three times, using a wide zigzag with a medium stitch length or a medium straight stitch. In the same way, attach the other pieces of ribbon to the front of the bra top about 2 inches out from each dart (Diagram 4).

Diagram 4

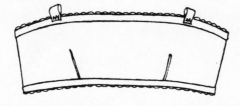

8. Use the remaining lingerie elastic to make the straps for the garment, following the instructions that are given in Project 9, step 8.

Project 12
Long-Leg Panty Girdle

Here is a figure-skimmer that will save as many dollars as it removes inches from your third vital statistic. It is easy to make, and, with its lace panels, it's really a pretty thing. We made it in daffodil colors because we were thinking of waist-wrapping, hip-hugging sundresses, but you could just as easily make it in black to give an absolutely devastating look to your best black knit. Choose whatever color tickles your color fancy, and help yourself become the body you always wanted to be. Then, make up the garment with a zigzag stitch—a straight stitch may not hold. If you don't have a zigzag machine, try using three rows of straight stitching on each seam, all the while stretching the fabric as much as possible. You may also use a stretch stitch if your machine is equipped with it.

MATERIALS NEEDED:

½ yard Lycra spandex, 44 inches wide
⅓ yard lace paneling, 9 inches wide
⅛ yard nylon tricot, 20 inches wide
1 yard lingerie plush elastic, ¾ inch wide
1¼ yards stretch lace, 1 to 2 inches wide
nylon lingerie thread

TOOLS NEEDED:

pattern paper
scissors
transparent tape
ballpoint pins
#9 ballpoint sewing-machine needle

PROCEDURE:

1. Measure your hips and waist to determine your size according to
the chart below.

small	*medium*	*large*
waist 24–26 inches	26–28 inches	28–30 inches
hips 35–37 inches	37–39 inches	39–41 inches

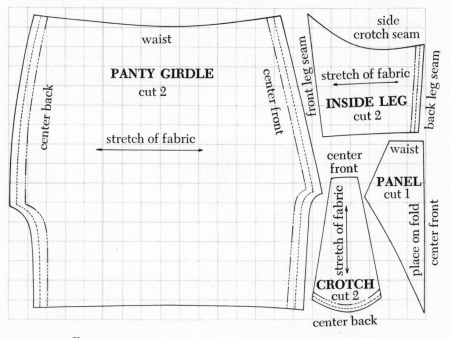

_.....small
.........medium
_____large

each square = 1 inch

Then enlarge all four pattern pieces to size on the pattern paper (page 17), transfer any pattern markings, cut out the pieces, and label them.

2. Preshrink the tricot piece before you begin. Then fold the Lycra, right sides together, so that the selvage edges meet. Place the main pattern piece and the inner leg pattern on top, positioning them so that the greatest amount of stretch will go around the body. Cut out the pieces. Mark the front and back inside leg seams of both leg pieces with tape and write on each piece of tape "front" or "back." Next, fold the tricot so that you have a piece that measures ⅛ yard by 10 inches; place the crotch piece on top and cut out. (You have cut two of these so that both crotch seams can be enclosed.) Mark the right sides of all pieces with tape. Finally, cut one panel piece from the lace paneling.

3. With right sides together and using a narrow zigzag with a short stitch length (or a stretch stitch if your machine has one), join the center front seam, allowing a ¼-inch seam allowance. Open the seam flat and topstitch down the center, using a wide zigzag with a medium stitch length.

4. With the right side of the lace panel against the wrong side of the girdle, align the center of the panel with the center front seam; pin in place. Now, turn the girdle over to the right side and, using a wide zigzag and medium stitch length, topstitch around the edge of the lace paneling, which will show through the Lycra. Cut away the Lycra inside the topstitching about ¼ inch in all around. Topstitch around the edge of the Lycra (Diagram 1).

Diagram 1

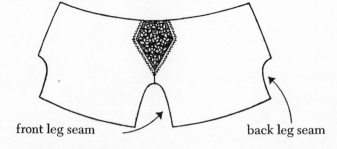

front leg seam   back leg seam

5. With the right sides together, join the center back seam and top-stitch it, as described in step 3.

6. Now add the crotch section to the girdle. The straight long edges of the crotch pieces are the inner leg seams. With the right sides together, place this edge of one crotch piece against the longer, curved edge (crotch seam) of one inner leg piece (Diagram 2). The back

Diagram 2

of the crotch piece should be at the back leg seam. Place the right side of the *other* crotch piece against the *wrong* side of the leg piece, matching its position with the first crotch piece so that there are three thicknesses at the inner leg crotch seam. Using a narrow zigzag stitch with a short stitch length, join the inner leg seam, using a ¼-inch seam allowance. Do not trim the seam.

7. To make the other enclosed crotch seam, place the unattached edge of one of the crotch pieces on the longer, curved edge of the *other* leg piece, right sides together (Diagram 3). Roll the Lycra up

Diagram 3

and bring the other crotch piece around to the crotch seam. The right side of the crotch piece will now be against the wrong side of the other leg piece (Diagram 4). With a narrow zigzag and short stitch length, sew a ¼-inch crotch seam; pull out the Lycra pieces. Topstitch both crotch seams, using a wide zigzag with a medium-length stitch (Diagram 5).

Diagram 4

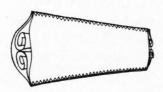

Diagram 5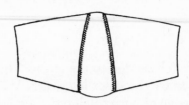

8. With right sides together, pin the center back of the crotch piece to the center back seam of the girdle (Diagram 6). Sew the back leg seam and then topstitch, following the instructions in step 3.

Diagram 6

9. Before sewing the front leg seams, add the stretch lace to the edges of the leg openings. Cut two pieces of stretch lace to the same measurement as the leg of the girdle. With the bottom edge of the lace even with the Lycra edge, tape the top edge, right side up, along the right side of the leg openings, being careful not to stretch the lace. Topstitch it at the top edge of the lace, using a wide zigzag with a medium stitch length. Trim the Lycra from behind the lace to help prevent the girdle from riding up the leg.

10. Pin the center of the front of the crotch piece to the center front seam, right sides together. Sew the front crotch seam and then top-stitch it, as described in step 3.

11. Cut a piece of plush elastic ½ inch longer than the waist measurement of the girdle. Overlap the ends by about ½ inch and join them by hand whipstitching or machine zigzagging. Place the seam at the back seam of the girdle, with the elastic on the right side of the girdle, the plush side up, and the picot trim pointing down. Using a narrow zigzag stitch with a short stitch length, sew along the picot edge of the elastic, stretching the elastic and the Lycra slightly as you sew.

12. Turn the elastic to the inside of the girdle. The picot trim should be pointing up. Topstitch ¼ inch in from the top edge of the right side of the girdle, again stretching the elastic and girdle slightly as you sew and using a wide zigzag stitch with a medium stitch length.

Project 13
Panty Brief Girdle

With the gentle control this panty brief girdle exercises over the tummy and hips, it gives a smoother, sleeker look to practically any body under practically any clothing. On a thin figure, it can work wonders; on a more rounded figure, it will help. It won't, however, replace the long-legged panty girdle, for it simply will not smooth out those lumps and bumps as gracefully. It will suffice, though, for most bodies and most clothing. Look for the two-way stretch fabric used in this project in the swimwear or body-suit fabric area. If you don't have a zigzag feature on your sewing machine, you can try using three rows of straight stitching down each side of each seam, stretching the fabric as much as possible while you are sewing.

MATERIALS NEEDED:

½ yard two-way stretch fabric, 86- to 87-percent nylon and
    13- to 14-percent Lycra spandex, 42 inches wide
1½ yards lingerie plush elastic, ⅜ to ½ inch wide
nylon lingerie thread

TOOLS NEEDED:

pattern paper
scissors
ballpoint pins
#9 ballpoint sewing-machine needle

each square = 1 inch

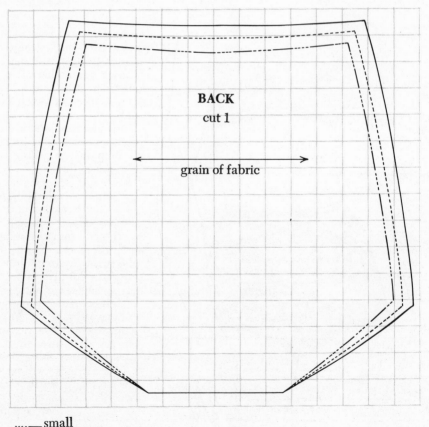

BACK
cut 1

grain of fabric

.... small
------ medium
_____ large

PROCEDURE:

1. To determine the pattern size you should use, measure your hips and compare the result with the chart below.

small	*medium*	*large*
34–36 inches	36–38 inches	38–40 inches

Enlarge the two pattern pieces to size on the pattern paper (page 17), transfer any pattern markings, cut out the pieces, and label them.

2. Lay the fabric out flat and place the pattern pieces on it, making sure to position them so that the grain of the fabric will go around your hips. Cut out the pieces.

each square = 1 inch

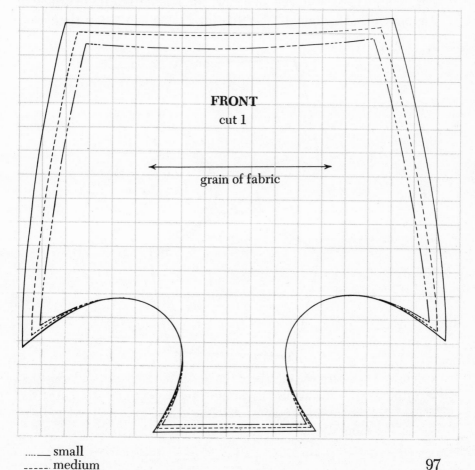

FRONT
cut 1

← grain of fabric →

......__ small
_____ medium
____ large

3. With the right sides together (the shiny, silky sides), join the front to the back at the crotch seam, using the rolled seam method—a wide zigzag stitch with a short stitch length.

4. For the leg openings, cut two pieces of elastic that are 14½ inches long for a small size, 15½ for a medium, and 16½ for a large. (The elastic will be slightly shorter than the leg openings.) Mark the midpoint of the elastic pieces and of the leg openings. With the elastic on the right side of the panty, the picot edge pointing in toward the fabric, and the plush side up, match the midpoint of one elastic piece with the midpoint of one leg opening; pin in place. Make sure that the straight edge of the elastic is even with the edge of the panty fabric. Starting at the side seam and sewing next to the picot edge with a narrow zigzag and short stitch length, add the elastic to the opening (Diagram 1). Stretch the elastic and panty slightly as

Diagram 1

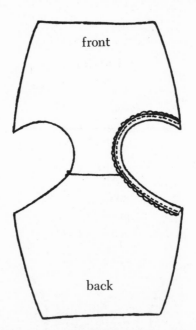

front

back

you sew. Then turn the elastic to the inside of the panty and topstitch it, using a wide zigzag and medium stitch length and stretching the elastic and the fabric as you go. Add the elastic to the other leg opening in the same way.

5. With the right sides together, join one side seam with a rolled seam. Use a wide zigzag and short stitch length for this. Begin sewing at the waist and stitch through the leg elastic when you come to it.

6. For the waist elastic, cut one piece of plush elastic 18 inches long for a small size, 19 inches for a medium, and 20 for a large. Divide the panty top into quarters; mark with pins. Now quarter the elastic and mark the divisions with pins. Place the elastic on the right side of the panty with the picot edge pointing down, the straight edge even with the panty top, and the plush side up (Diagram 2). Then match the

Diagram 2

pins in the panty top with the pins in the elastic. Starting at the open side seam, sew along the picot edge, using a narrow zigzag and short stitch length. Stretch the elastic to fit the panty top and then stretch the elastic and the panty top as you sew.

7. Turn the elastic to the inside of the panty and topstitch it on the right side of the panty, using a wide zigzag and medium stitch length. Stretch the elastic and the panty as you sew. When you are finished, the plush side of the elastic should be on the inside of the panty where it will protect the skin when the panty is worn.

8. Join the remaining side seam, using the rolled seam technique—a wide zigzag with a short stitch length. Begin sewing at the waist and stitch through both the waist elastic and the leg elastic.

Project 14
Body Briefer

Here's a skinny little body suit—tank-top style—that's made of Lycra spandex for the best figure shaping around. If you want to make a real body skimmer without the control element, use a two-way stretch nylon—try it in all twenty or thirty terrific colors it now comes in and wear them under filmy overthings, use them to create the high-fashion layered look, or coordinate them with a group of wraparound skirts. You might also try this style in one of the stretchy swimsuit fabrics, which are more likely to be patterned. You could then tie a scarf around your hair and take off for the beach—a classic as flattering as this one will put all the bikinis right out to sea.

MATERIALS NEEDED:

¾ yard Lycra spandex, 38 inches wide, preferably lightweight
2½ yards stretch lace, ⅜ to ½ inch wide
7 inches seam binding, ⅝ inch wide, for crotch reinforcement
four snaps, #2/0 size
nylon lingerie thread

TOOLS NEEDED:

pattern paper
scissors
transparent tape
ballpoint pins
#9 ballpoint sewing-machine needle

PROCEDURE:

1. Measure your bust and hips to determine your correct size according to the chart below.

small	medium	large
bust 32 inches	34 inches	36 inches
hips 34–36 inches	36–38 inches	38–40 inches

Enlarge the three pattern pieces on the pattern paper (page 17),

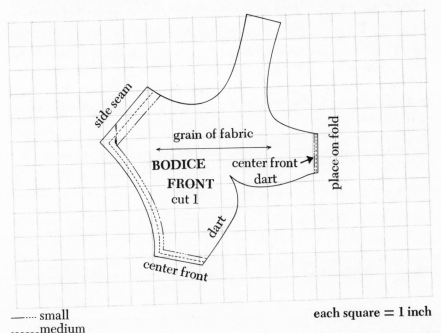

side seam

grain of fabric

place on fold

BODICE FRONT
cut 1

center front →
dart

dart

center front

—···· small
------medium
——large

each square = 1 inch

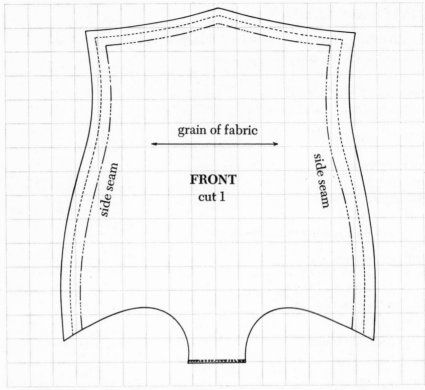

grain of fabric

FRONT
cut 1

side seam

side seam

transfer any pattern markings, cut out the pieces, and label them.

2. Lay the Lycra out flat and cut one each of the front and back pieces, making certain that the grain and greatest amount of stretch go around the body. Fold the remaining Lycra on the crosswise grain, right sides together. Lay the center front fold of the bodice front pattern piece on the fold of the Lycra; cut out. Then mark the right sides of all pieces with tape.

3. With the right sides together, join the center front seam of the bodice, using a narrow zigzag with a short stitch length (Diagram 1).

Diagram 1

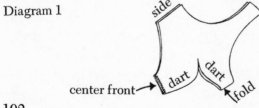

center front →

side

dart   dart

fold

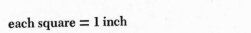

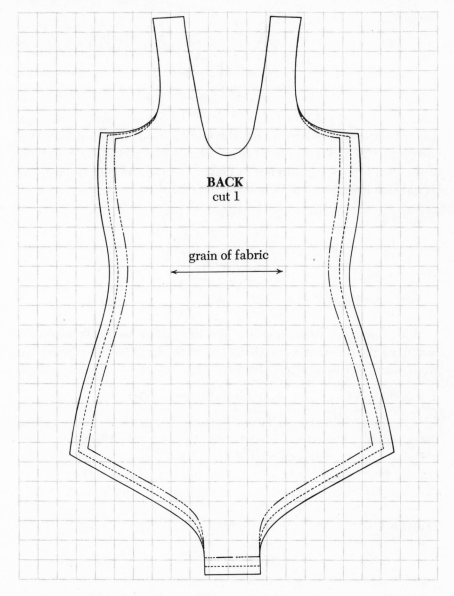

BACK
cut 1

grain of fabric

Use this stitch for all the sewing in this project except for the seam binding at the crotch, and sew ¼-inch seams.

4. Open the bodice and fold it horizontally, right sides together, so that the edges of the dart seams meet (Diagram 2). The center front

Diagram 2

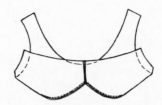

seam that you just stitched should be on the top side of the fold. Zig-zag the darts all the way across the bodice front, stitching over the end of the stitched center front seam. Backstitch carefully at each end of the dart to lock the stitches in place. The right side of the bodice should look like Diagram 3 when you have finished.

Diagram 3

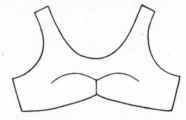

5. With the right sides together, join the bodice to the front piece, matching the side seams and the center of the front piece to the center front seam in the bodice (Diagram 4).

6. Join the front and back shoulder seams, right sides together.

7. Cut a piece of stretch lace 2 inches shorter than the neckline measurement. Overlap the ends slightly and join them by hand whipstitching or machine zigzagging. Turn the garment right side out and lay the lace, right side up, around the neckline. The seam in the lace should be at one of the shoulder seams, and about half the

Diagram 4

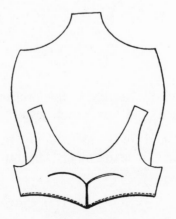

width of the lace should be extending over the edge of the Lycra. Then, starting at the seam in the lace, topstitch it, stretching the lace slightly as you sew.

8. Measure the armhole opening and cut two pieces of stretch lace 1 inch shorter than that measurement. Fold the lace pieces in half and mark the midpoints with pins. With the garment still right side out, pin the midpoint of the lace to one shoulder seam. The lace should be right side up and about half its width should extend over the edge of the armhole. Topstitch it in position, starting at the side seam and stretching the lace slightly to fit. Repeat to add the lace to the other armhole.

9. With the right sides together, join the side seams, stitching from the bottom to the top.

10. Measure one leg opening and cut two pieces of stretch lace 3 inches shorter than that measurement. Turn the garment right side out, and pin the lace in place at the front and back of the crotch on one leg opening. Turn under both ends of the piece of lace to hide the raw edges. Once again, about half the width of the lace should extend beyond the edge of the fabric. Topstitch, stretching the lace slightly on the front leg opening and more on the back leg opening to provide more fullness in the back, where it is needed. Now, topstitch the stretch lace to the other leg opening in the same way.

11. Cut the rayon seam binding in half and follow Diagram 5 while you are adding it to the crotch. With right sides together, fold the front crotch piece up about ½ inch and pin one length of seam binding across the edge. Fold each end under to fit the width of the crotch. With the wrong sides together, fold the edge of the back crotch piece up ½ inch and pin the remaining piece of seam binding across in the same manner. Stitch around the seam binding in a rectangular pattern, using a short straight stitch. Do this on both the front and the back pieces. Sew four snaps on the seam binding so that when they are snapped, the seam binding will come together.

Diagram 5

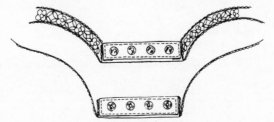

Project 15
Knee-length Half Slip

With skirts having recently returned to the fashion scene—and likely to remain there for some seasons to come—you've probably found your undies drawer sadly lacking in things to wear under them. The best solution is to make your own, a plan that will do more than just save money. It will enable you to have just the color you need, important in view of fashion's greatly expanded spectrum, and to choose a style as tailored or as elaborate as you wish. In this basic half slip project, we offer four or five such variations. And think of this: Making a slip is probably less time-consuming, certainly less frazzling, than is shopping for one.

MATERIALS NEEDED:

¾ yard nylon tricot, 54 inches wide
2 yards nylon lace, in width of your choice, for hemline (optional)
1 yard lingerie waist elastic, ½ inch wide
nylon lingerie *or* polyester thread

TOOLS NEEDED:

pattern paper
scissors
transparent tape
ballpoint pins
#9 ballpoint sewing-machine needle

PROCEDURE:

1. Before beginning, preshrink the tricot. Then measure your waist and hips to determine the pattern size you should use according to the chart below.

	small	*medium*	*large*
waist	24–26 inches	27–29 inches	30–32 inches
hips	35–37 inches	38–40 inches	41–43 inches

Enlarge the pattern piece to size on the pattern paper (page 17), transfer any pattern markings, cut out the piece, and label it.

2. Lay out the tricot and place the pattern on top, making certain that you place the grain line on the grain of the fabric. Cut out the front piece, reposition the pattern—without flopping it—and cut out the back pieces. After you have cut out both pieces, mark their right sides with tape.

3. With your machine set for a wide zigzag and a short stitch length, roll one side seam, right sides together, sewing along the edge of the seam so that the zigzag goes off the fabric. The seam should be stitched from top to bottom. If you don't have a zigzag, use a short straight stitch with a ¼-inch seam allowance and trim the seam after sewing, cutting close to the stitching.

4. If you wish to add lace to the hemline (see step 5 for alternatives),

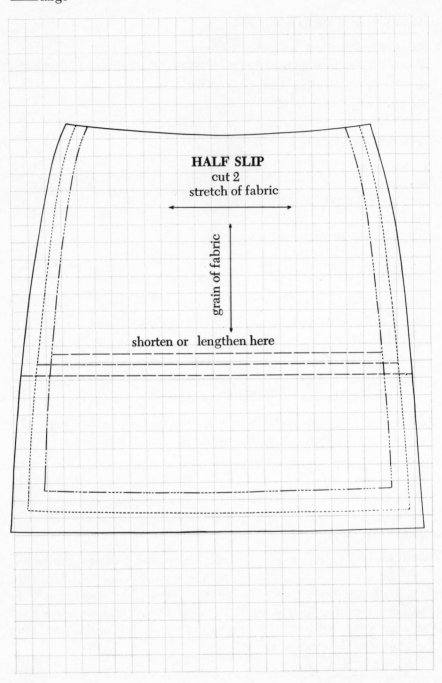

HALF SLIP
cut 2
stretch of fabric

grain of fabric

shorten or lengthen here

108

open the slip and lay it out flat on a flat surface, right side up. Remove the tape markers, place the bottom edge of the lace along the bottom edge of the slip with the right side up, and tape the lace in place along the top edge. If the lace is scalloped on one edge, that edge should be at the bottom. With a wide zigzag and medium-length stitch or a medium-length straight stitch, sew along the top edge of the lace. You can either leave the tricot behind the lace or trim it away at the seamline. If you leave it, do not sew the bottom of the lace to the tricot, as this may pucker the fabric.

5. If you wish, you can insert a length of lace an inch or two above the bottom edge of the slip and topstitch it in place along both its top and bottom edges. Then cut away the tricot from behind the lace, close to both seamlines. You can then turn under the bottom edge of the slip and decorate it with a fancy cam stitch, or you can just roll it, using the rolled seam technique. You might also apply another length of lace to the edge, as described in step 4. Or, for a more tailored look, you can omit the lace altogether, turn the bottom edge under to make a hem, and then decorate it with a fancy cam stitch.

6. Now join the other side seam as described in step 3. Sew from the top to the bottom and stitch through the lace. Don't forget to set your stitch length back to a short stitch. If you have cut away the tricot from behind the lace, topstitch over the seam in the lace to prevent it from pulling out.

7. Cut the elastic to 4 inches less than your waist measurement and add it to the top of the slip as described in Project 1, step 6.

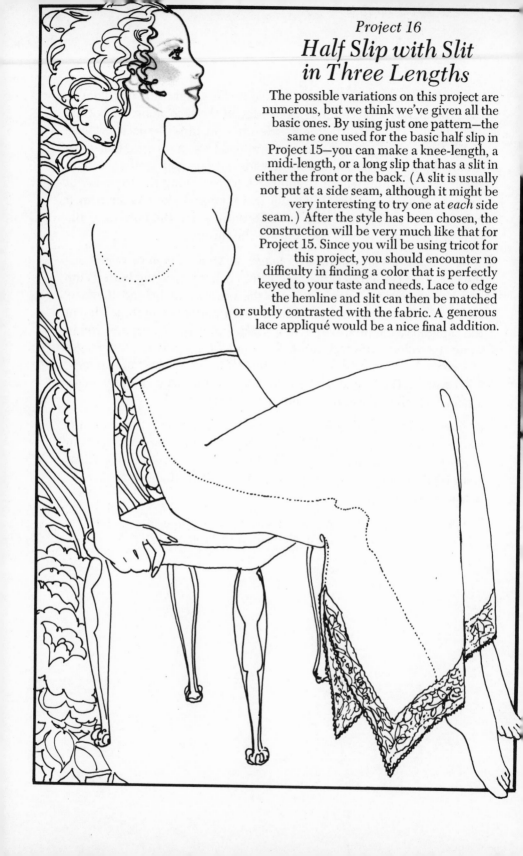

Half Slip with Slit in Three Lengths

The possible variations on this project are numerous, but we think we've given all the basic ones. By using just one pattern—the same one used for the basic half slip in Project 15—you can make a knee-length, a midi-length, or a long slip that has a slit in either the front or the back. (A slit is usually not put at a side seam, although it might be very interesting to try one at *each* side seam.) After the style has been chosen, the construction will be very much like that for Project 15. Since you will be using tricot for this project, you should encounter no difficulty in finding a color that is perfectly keyed to your taste and needs. Lace to edge the hemline and slit can then be matched or subtly contrasted with the fabric. A generous lace appliqué would be a nice final addition.

MATERIALS NEEDED:

1¼ yards nylon tricot, 54 inches wide (enough for long slip)
2 yards nylon lace, in width of your choice, for hemline (optional)
1 yard lingerie waist elastic, ½ inch wide
nylon lingerie *or* polyester thread

TOOLS NEEDED:

pattern paper
scissors
transparent tape
ballpoint pins
#9 ballpoint sewing-machine needle

PROCEDURE:

1. To make a knee-length half slip, use the pattern for Project 15 as is. If you wish a longer slip, cut the pattern on the cutting line and add the extra length between the pieces. Then do steps, 1, 2, and 3 of Project 15, but join both side seams instead of only one.

2. Decide where you would like the slit to be and fold the slip along that line, wrong sides together (Diagram 1); also decide on how

Diagram 1

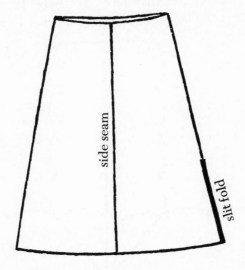

side seam

slit fold

long you would like the slit (for a knee-length slip, allow 6 to 8 inches; for a full-length slip, it should extend from the bottom edge to just below the knee). Measure off that distance on the fold and mark it with a pin. Then fold the lace in half so that the patterns on the front and back pieces match (Diagram 2); mark the fold with a pin. With

Diagram 2

that pin placed at the fold in the slip that is *opposite* to the slit fold, lay the lace along the bottom edge of the slip. The right side of the lace should be up, the lace should be applied to the right side of the slip, and the bottom edge of the lace should be even with the bottom edge of the slip. If one edge of the lace is scalloped, place that edge so that it points toward the top of the slip. Then hold the lace in place with strips of tape placed along its top edge. Mark the slit line with another strip of tape. Then, turn the slip over and continue to add the lace to the bottom edge in the same way.

3. Refold the slip so that the slit is in the center front. Fold the lace back and up, making sure that the edges meet at the slit line (Diagram 3). The ends of the lace should extend about 2 inches above the pin

Diagram 3

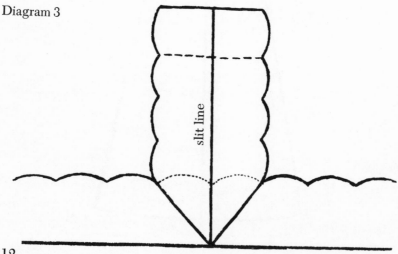

slit line

that is marking the top of the slit. The ends of the lace can either be folded under and left with a straight edge, or they can be mitered. To miter them, fold the ends over to meet the straight edge of the lace along the slit line (Diagram 4). Using a wide zigzag and medium

Diagram 4

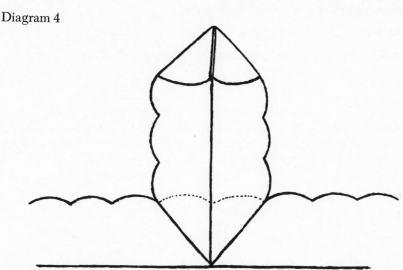

stitch length or a medium straight stitch, add the lace to the slip by sewing along its top edge all around and around the triangle at the bottom of the slit. Sew both sides of the lace at the slit and across the top (Diagram 5).

Diagram 5

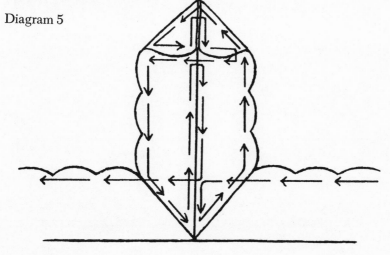

4. After the lace is sewn in place, slit the fabric between the pieces of lace. If you wish to trim the tricot from behind the lace at the hemline, do not sew through the tricot when you are sewing the triangles at the bottom of the slit. To reinforce the top of the slit, you may use a lace appliqué, but it isn't necessary.

5. Cut the elastic to 4 inches less than your waist measurement and add it to the top in the same way as described in Project 1, step 6.

Project 17

Peasant Petticoat

This gay peasant-style petticoat with its flouncy ruffle is reminiscent of the last century in the world's back country. In spirit, it is as much American pioneer as it is Bohemian gypsy or Portuguese peasant. If you have a full skirt, wear three or four of these slips under it—nothing is quite so appealing as yards and yards of lace-edged ruffle peeking out below a hemline. If you wish, dye the slips in monochromatic tones and layer them in order of color intensity. Or fashion both the slip and the camisole on page 147 of a printed cotton or a lightweight wool challis for unique spring and summer dressing

MATERIALS NEEDED:

2¼ yards batiste, Indian gauze, or broadcloth (combination
    cotton and polyester), 45 inches wide
1½ yards polyester–cotton lace trim, ⅜ inch wide
1 yard lingerie waist elastic, ½ inch wide
polyester thread

TOOLS NEEDED:

pattern paper
scissors
straight pins
#9 sewing-machine needle

PROCEDURE:

1. Wash the fabric so that it will be preshrunk. Measure your waist
and hips to determine your size according to the chart below:

	small	medium	large
waist	24–26 inches	27–29 inches	30–32 inches
hips	35–37 inches	38–40 inches	41–43 inches

Then, enlarge the pattern piece to size on the pattern paper (page
17), transfer any pattern markings, cut out the piece, and label it.

2. Fold the fabric on the crosswise grain and place the pattern on it,
making sure to follow the pattern markings for grain lines since this
fabric has no stretch (Diagram 1). Cut out. Then cut a length of

Diagram 1

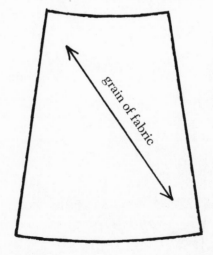

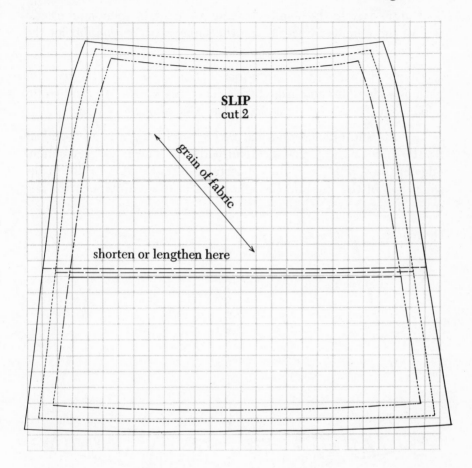

SLIP
cut 2

grain of fabric

shorten or lengthen here

fabric that is 4½ inches wide and 52 inches long for the ruffle. This does not have to be cut on the bias, and it may be pieced at the side seams if necessary.

3. Join one side seam by placing the front and back sections right sides together and stitching with a wide zigzag and a short stitch length or a short straight stitch.

4. Turn one edge of the ruffle under ¼ inch and press it; then turn another ¼ inch under and press again. Using a wide zigzag with a medium stitch length or a medium straight stitch, topstitch it to make a hem.

5. Add the lace to the hem by placing it right side up along the right side of the hemmed edge. Using the same stitch as you did for the hem, topstitch it in place.

6. Divide the ruffle into four equal sections and mark the divisions with pins along the unfinished edge. Then, with your machine set for a long straight stitch, stitch along that edge about ¼ inch in.

7. Lay the slip out flat on a flat surface. With right sides together, lay the ruffle on top so that its unfinished edge is even with the bottom edge of the slip. Place the pin marking the center of the ruffle at the side seam of the slip and the other pins at the midpoint of the slip front, the midpoint of the slip back, and the side edge (Diagram 2).

Diagram 2

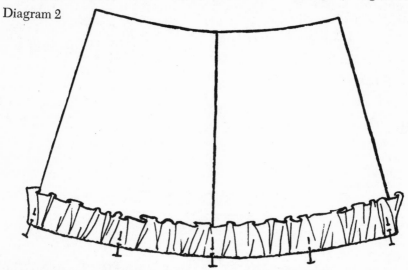

Pull on the threads to gather it evenly. When the gathers are equally distributed around the bottom of the slip, join the ruffle to the slip. Use a narrow zigzag with a short stitch length or a short straight stitch; allow a ¼-inch seam allowance.

8. Stitch the other side seam, sewing through the ruffle and using a wide zigzag with a short stitch length or a short straight stitch.

9. To add the waistband elastic, follow Project 1, step 6.

Project 18
Bias-cut Full Slip

One of the best things
about this slip is that it
can be made of practically
any lightweight woven
fabric. Unless you change
the grain line on the
pattern to run from
the top to the bottom
instead of diagonally,
knit fabrics, including
tricot, should
be avoided, for they will
add too much stretch to the pieces. We
chose sheath lining for our slip because
there were so many pretty colors
available, but you might try a rustly
taffeta, a cheery calico, or even an
old-fashioned soft flannel with eyelet
trim. You can lengthen this pattern
simply by adding the desired amount to
the bottom, continuing the flare as you
add. You need not add a slit unless you
want to; if you do, see the instructions in
Project 16. If you wish to make a long
slip, buy an extra yard of fabric.

MATERIALS NEEDED:

1⅜ yards woven fabric, 45 inches wide (enough for short slip)
½ yard nylon lace with one scalloped edge, 3½ to 4 inches wide,
  for front bodice
1 yard nylon lace, ⅜ to ½ inch wide, for top back and side edges
2 yards nylon lace, width of your choice, for hemline
2 slip straps, either commercially made or homemade
6 inches nylon sheer, ½ inch wide (optional)
nylon lingerie *or* polyester thread

TOOLS NEEDED:

pattern paper
scissors
transparent tape
straight pins
#9 sewing-machine needle

PROCEDURE:

1. Preshrink the fabric before you begin. Then measure your bust and hips to determine your proper size according to the chart below.

	small	*medium*	*large*
bust	32 inches	34 inches	36 inches
hips	34–36 inches	36–38 inches	38–40 inches

Enlarge the four pattern pieces to the proper size on the pattern paper (page 17), transfer all pattern markings, cut out the pieces, and label them.

2. Lay out the fabric and place on it the patterns for the front piece, the back piece, and the lower front bodice piece. Cut one of each and then flip over the patterns for the back piece and the lower front bodice piece; cut one more of each. Cut the upper front bodice piece from the wide nylon lace: Fold the lace in half, wrong sides together, so that the designs on the front and back sides match and then lay the pattern on top, with the scalloped edge of the pattern on the scalloped edge of the lace; cut out.

3. With the right sides together, sew one piece of bodice lace to one of

120

each square = 1 inch

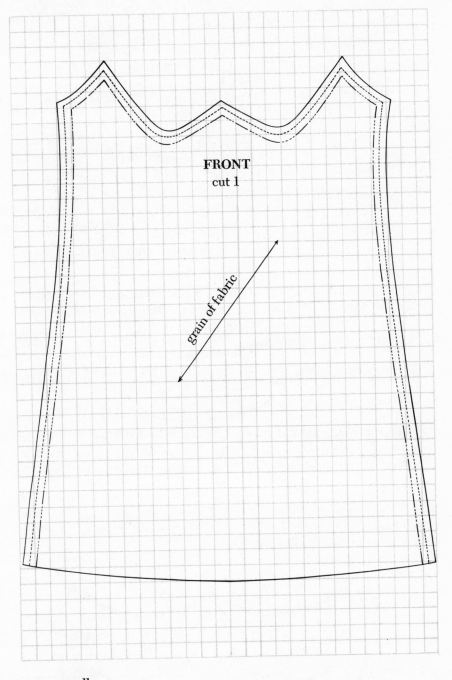

FRONT
cut 1

grain of fabric

------- small
--------- medium
———— large

121

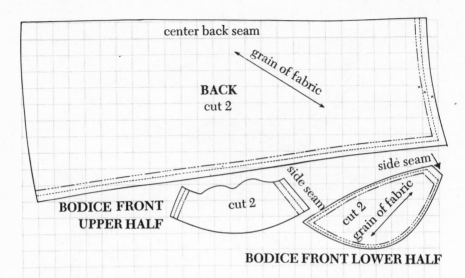

center back seam

BACK
cut 2

grain of fabric

BODICE FRONT
UPPER HALF

cut 2

side seam

side seam

cut 2

grain of fabric

BODICE FRONT LOWER HALF

the lower front bodice pieces, using a wide zigzag with a short stitch length to make a rolled seam (Diagram 1). (Remember that the right side of the lace is the side with the raised thread.) If you don't have

Diagram 1

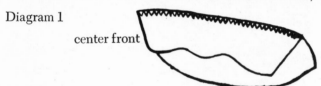

center front

a zigzag machine, use a short straight stitch and sew a ¼-inch seam. Join the other lace piece with the other bodice piece, making sure that you have both a right and a left bodice front when you are finished.

4. Place the right sides of each front bodice piece against the right side of the slip front and sew a rolled seam, stitching from each side to the center (Diagram 2). You may also use a short straight stitch with a ¼-inch seam allowance.

Diagram 2

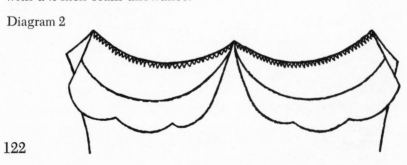

5. Join the center front seam of the bodice with the right sides together. Start stitching at the top of the lace and sew to the point at the center of the slip front, using the rolled seam method or a short straight stitch with a ¼-inch seam allowance (Diagram 3).

Diagram 3

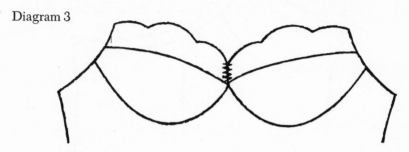

6. Join the side seams, right sides together, sewing from the bottom of the slip to the top, using the rolled seam technique or a short straight stitch with a ¼-inch seam allowance. Be careful not to stretch the fabric—since this slip was cut on the bias, any stretching will result in a wavy seam. Press both seams with a warm iron; if there are any ripples in the seams, careful pressing may work them out.

7. Place the slip on a flat surface, right side up. Tape the top edge of the hemline lace to the bottom of the slip so that the bottom edges are even. Using a wide zigzag and medium stitch length or a medium straight stitch, sew along the top edge of the lace, removing the tape before you get to it or after the seam has been sewn. Be careful not to stretch the fabric as you sew. Then trim the fabric behind the lace close to the stitching.

8. Join the back seam of the slip, right sides together, using the rolled seam technique or a short straight stitch with a ¼-inch seam allowance. Stitch from the bottom of the hemline lace to the top of the slip. The lace seam may be topstitched for extra strength if you wish.

9. Measure off 1½ inches from one end of the narrow lace and mark with a pin. (This extra lace will be used when attaching the slip straps.) Place the pin in the lace at the top edge of the left front bodice lace (Diagram 4). The wrong side of the lace should be

123

Diagram 4

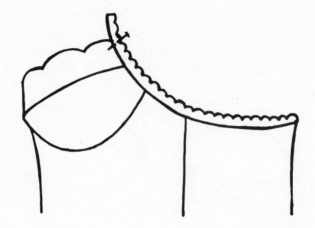

against the right side of the slip, and the bottom edge of the lace should overlap the top edge of the slip by about ¼ inch. Tape the bottom edge of the lace around the sides and back of the slip top. Cut the lace at the right bodice 1½ inches longer than is needed. Being careful not to stretch the fabric and keeping the lace taut, topstitch along the bottom edge of the lace, using a narrow zigzag stitch with a short stitch length or a short straight stitch.

10. If you wish to make your own slip straps, follow the directions given on page 23. Then place the back ends of the straps at the x's on the slip back, placing them behind the lace and overlapping the top edge of the fabric (Diagram 5). With a medium zigzag stitch

Diagram 5

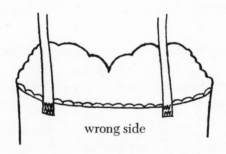

wrong side

and medium stitch length or a medium straight stitch, topstitch two or three times over them to hold them firmly in place. Place the front ends of the straps at the bodice front behind the lace edging. Fold the extra 1½ inches of lace to the back of each strap (Diagram 6), and

Diagram 6

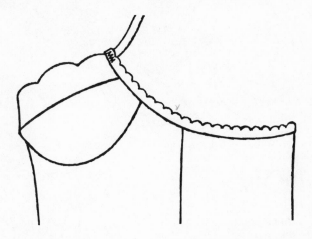

topstitch them in place. If the straps are not adjustable, try on the slip first and pin the front ends to the length that is comfortable.

11. A small bow made from nylon sheer can be sewn at the center point of the slip; follow the directions given on page 27.

Project 19
Chemise Slip

There are but two pattern pieces for this quick and easy chemise-style slip, which makes it an excellent choice as immediate filler for your slip wardrobe. Because it fits the body very loosely, it is exceptionally easy and cool to wear. However, it does not lend itself well to body-clinging or closely tailored garments. It does do well under tent dresses and shirred-yoke dresses, with or without waist ties. It also makes up well as summer nightwear. As an experiment, try it in a fairly sturdy cotton knit and wear it as a jumper over a voile blouse or a T-shirt. Make the straps of the same fabric. If you want to make this slip knee-length, simply add the extra amount to the bottom of the pattern and buy a bit of extra fabric. If you make it any longer, you will probably have to add a slit.

MATERIALS NEEDED:

1 yard nylon tricot, 52 inches wide
2½ yards nylon lace, 1 to 2 inches wide
2 slip straps, either commercially made or homemade
nylon lingerie *or* polyester thread

TOOLS NEEDED:

pattern paper
scissors
transparent tape
ballpoint pins
#9 ballpoint sewing-machine needle

PROCEDURE:

1. Wash the tricot so that it will be preshrunk. Then measure your bust and hips to determine your proper size according to the chart below.

	small	*medium*	*large*
bust	32 inches	34 inches	36 inches
hips	34–36 inches	36–38 inches	38–40 inches

Then enlarge the two pattern pieces on the pattern paper (page 17), transfer any pattern markings, cut out the pieces, and label them.

2. Lay out the tricot, place the pattern pieces on top so that the stretch of the fabric will go around the body, and cut them out. Mark their right sides with tape.

3. Using a wide zigzag and short stitch length to make a rolled seam or a short straight stitch with a ¼-inch seam allowance, sew the darts in the front of the slip. Then join one side seam in the same way, stitching from the bottom to the top and stretching the fabric slightly as you go.

4. Place the slip, right side up, out flat on a flat surface and tape the lace, right side up, to the top and bottom edges of the slip (Diagram 1). The edges of the lace should be even with the edges of the tricot.

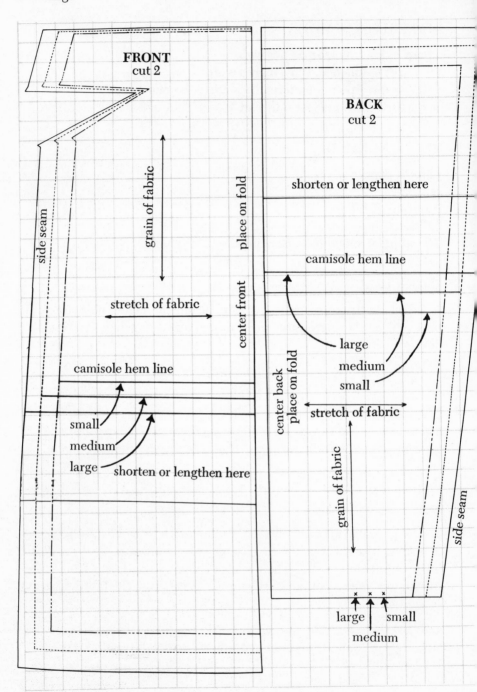

FRONT
cut 2

grain of fabric

side seam

place on fold

center front

stretch of fabric

camisole hem line

small
medium
large

shorten or lengthen here

BACK
cut 2

shorten or lengthen here

camisole hem line

large
medium
small

center back
place on fold

stretch of fabric

grain of fabric

side seam

large   small

Diagram 1

With a wide zigzag and medium stitch length or a medium straight stitch, topstitch along the top edge of the lace at the bottom of the slip and along the bottom edge of the lace at the top of the slip. Remove the tape before you come to it or after you have stitched through it. Then trim away the tricot from behind the lace at both the top and bottom of the slip, cutting close to the topstitching.

5. Place the right sides of the slip together and roll the other side seam or use a short straight stitch with a ¼-inch seam allowance. Sew from the bottom to the top.

6. If you wish to make your own slip straps, follow the instructions given on page 23; otherwise use commercially made straps. Place the back ends of the straps at the x's; the straps should be behind the lace and the ends should just touch the tricot. Using a wide zigzag and medium stitch length or a medium straight stitch, topstitch across the strap at the bottom and the top edge of the lace to fasten it securely (Diagram 2). If you are using nonadjustable straps, try on

Diagram 2

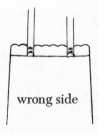

wrong side

the slip and pin the front ends to the slip front to whatever length is comfortable; trim any extra length. Then topstitch them in place.

Project 20

Cami-Knickers

This nice bit of undies nostalgia was originally nurtured during the late thirties, when it might have been made of slinky peach satin, edged with hand-crocheted lace, and worn over the subtle curves of a platinum-haired Hollywood glamour queen. Not surprisingly, contemporary women have rediscovered them, finding them just as exciting as they were then, and cami-knickers are suddenly staging a full-scale comeback. Cami-knickers can be—and, traditionally, should be—worn simply as a coverall, without figure shapers. The result is a totally natural look that is still perfectly understated. And because nothing binds, they are the easiest of undies to wear—once you've tried them, you'll not be without. We've made ours of tricot, but you might try recycling a luscious antique satin or silk for them.

MATERIALS NEEDED:

¾ yard nylon tricot, 54 inches wide
3 yards nylon lace with both edges scalloped and a
    double floral design, 3½ inches wide
3 snaps, #3/0 size, for crotch fastening
nylon lingerie *or* polyester thread

TOOLS NEEDED:
pattern paper
scissors
transparent tape
ballpoint pins
#9 ballpoint sewing-machine needle

PROCEDURE:

1. Shrink the tricot before you begin working. Then measure your bust
and hips to determine your correct size according to the chart below.

	small	*medium*	*large*
bust	32 inches	34 inches	36 inches
hips	34–36 inches	36–38 inches	38–40 inches

Then enlarge the pattern pieces to size on the pattern paper (page
17), transfer any pattern markings, cut out the pieces, and label them.

2. Lay out the tricot and place the front and back pattern pieces on it.
Cut one of each, flip the patterns over, and cut another of each. Mark
their right sides with strips of transparent tape. Then fold the lace in
half with the wrong sides together and with the floral designs matching on both sides. Lay the three cup pieces on top and cut out. Last,
cut one back lace piece, using the back lace pattern. (You should have
enough lace left over to make the trim for the leg openings.)

3. Lay the lace cup pieces out in front of you so that you have a right
and a left cup (Diagram 1). Working with either cup first, lay the

Diagram 1

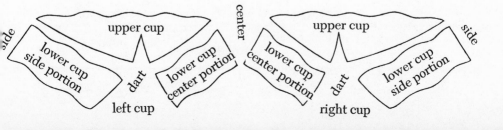

each square = 1 inch

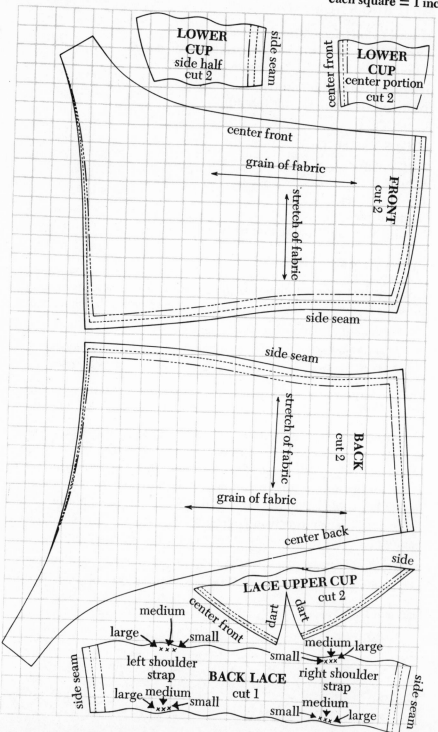

LOWER CUP side half cut 2

side seam

center front

LOWER CUP center portion cut 2

center front

grain of fabric

FRONT cut 2

stretch of fabric

side seam

side seam

stretch of fabric

BACK cut 2

grain of fabric

center back

side

LACE UPPER CUP cut 2

center front

dart

dart

medium

large small

medium large

small

left shoulder strap

right shoulder strap

side seam

BACK LACE cut 1

large medium small

medium small large

side seam

top edge of the side half of the lower cup on top of the bottom edge of the upper cup; both pieces should be right side up and the lower cup piece should overlap the upper cup by about ¼ inch. Topstitch around the scallops with a narrow zigzag stitch and short stitch length or a short straight stitch (Diagram 2). Trim the lower edge of the upper

Diagram 2

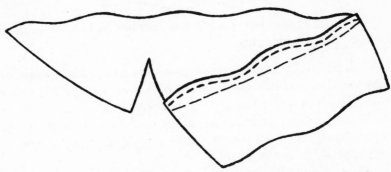

cup piece close to the topstitching. Lay the top edge of the other lower cup half over the other bottom edge of the upper cup in the same way and repeat the procedure (Diagram 3). Repeat for the other cup, making sure that you have both a right and a left cup.

Diagram 3

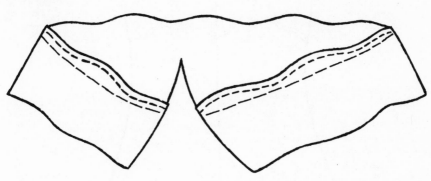

4. With the right sides together, fold one cup together at the dart and roll the dart seam, using a wide zigzag and short stitch length or a short straight stitch with a ¼-inch seam (Diagram 4). Sew from the bottom to the top. At the top of the dart, leave the needle in the lace,

Diagram 4

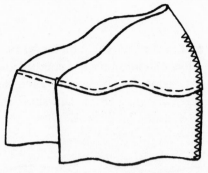

turn the fabric, and sew back a few stitches to lock them in place. Repeat for the other cup.

5. With the right sides together, place the center front edges of the cups together and join the seam, using a narrow zigzag with a short stitch length or a short straight stitch with a ¼-inch seam. Press the seam open and topstitch down the center of the seam with a wide zigzag and medium stitch length or use a medium straight stitch down each side of the center seam.

6. With their right sides together, place the two front tricot pieces together and roll the center front seam or sew a ¼-inch seam with a short straight stitch. Sew from the bottom to the top.

Diagram 5

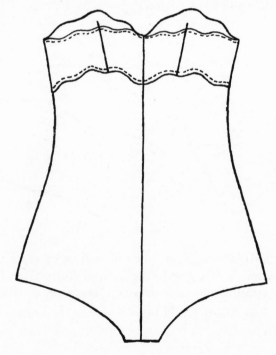

7. Lap the bottom edge of the lace cups over the top edge of the tricot front piece by about ⅜ inch—both pieces should be right side up and the center front seams should match (Diagram 5). Hold the pieces in place with tape. Using a narrow zigzag stitch with a short stitch length or a short straight stitch, topstitch around the scalloped edge of the lace, removing the tape before you come to it or after it has been stitched. Trim away the tricot that is behind the lace, cutting close to the topstitching.

8. With right sides together, place the two back tricot pieces together and roll the center back seam or sew it with a short straight stitch and allow a ¼-inch seam.

9. Tape the bottom edge of the lace back piece over the top edge of the tricot back piece about ⅜ inch (Diagram 6). Both sections should

Diagram 6

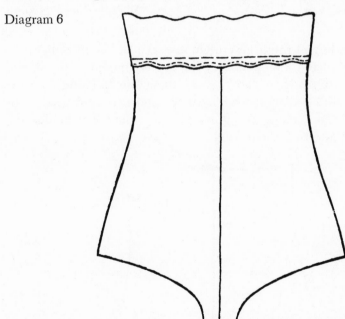

be right side up. Topstitch around the scalloped edge of the lace, using a narrow zigzag and short stitch length or a short straight stitch. Trim away the tricot behind the lace, cutting close to the topstitching.

10. Place the right side of the front piece against the right side of the

135

back and roll the side seams or sew with a ¼-inch seam and a short straight stitch. Sew from the bottom to the top, making certain that the lace trim on the top front and back pieces meet exactly. With the needle still in the lace, turn the fabric and sew back a few stitches to lock the stitching in place.

11. To make the lace trim for the leg openings, cut the lace in half, following the scalloped floral design (Diagram 7). Starting at the back

Diagram 7

crotch and ending at the front crotch, tape the lace, right side up, to the right side of the leg openings. The top edge of the lace should overlap the bottom edge of the tricot by about ⅜ inch. Using a narrow zigzag stitch with a short stitch length or a short straight stitch, top-stitch around the scallops (Diagram 8). Trim the tricot behind the lace, cutting close to the stitching.

Diagram 8

136

12. Press the edges of the front crotch piece and back crotch piece under ½ inch and topstitch, using a narrow zigzag with a short stitch length or a short straight stitch. Sew three snaps at the crotch, one at the center front and back seams and one at each leg opening (Diagram 9).

Diagram 9

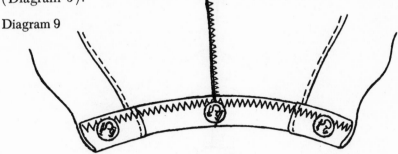

13. Make two spaghetti shoulder straps and bow according to the instructions on page 25. Each should measure about 18 inches long. Then place the back ends of the straps at the x's, on the wrong side of the lace and with the ends slightly below the bottom edge of the lace trim (Diagram 10). Zigzag or straight stitch across the strap at the

Diagram 10

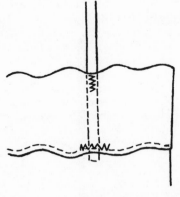

topstitching, turn the fabric with the needle still in it, and sew back a few stitches to reinforce. Also attach the strap to the top of the back lace: Start at the top of the lace and sew along the strap ½ inch; turn the garment and sew back to the top.

14. Try on the garment to find the most comfortable length for the

straps. Then place the front ends of the straps above the darts and about ½ inch below the top edge of the wrong side of the lace (Diagram 11). Starting at the end of the strap and stopping at the top of

Diagram 11

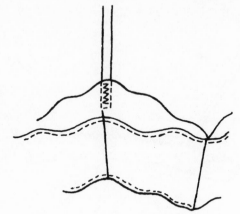

the lace, attach by stitching it with a narrow zigzag and short stitch length or a short straight stitch. With the needle still in the fabric, turn the garment and sew back to the end of the strap to reinforce the attachment. Trim away any extra strap length.

15. To add the spaghetti bow in front, place the midpoint of the spaghetti trim at the bottom of the lace cups and along the center front seamline (Diagram 12). Sew across the trim at the point where

Diagram 12

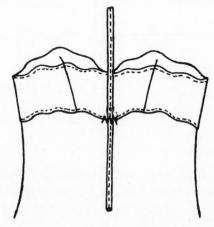

the lace is topstitched, using a narrow zigzag with a short stitch length or a short straight stitch. Tie the two ends into a bow.

Project 21

Slip-style Camisole

This short and very sweet
camisole topping is fashioned
like a full slip with a lace-trimmed
bodice. Made of tricot, it stretches
just enough to cling to the body
in a way that provides the
smoothest of lines under clothing,
and its stretch lace straps
reemphasize that flawlessness.
They also offer the very most in
wearing comfort. An extremely
practical adventure in undies
making, this camisole will entice
the penny watcher as well, for it
should cost less than two dollars
to make, depending on where you
buy your fabrics. For a real
come-hither look—and as a
reward for all those practical
undies endeavors—make it all of
lace. Or try a daisy-flocked cotton
to brighten even a sunshiny day.
A fresh white dimity or dotted
Swiss could be just as
rejuvenating to the spirit.

MATERIALS NEEDED:

½ yard nylon tricot, 44 inches wide
1½ yards nylon lace, 1 to 2 inches wide
1 yard stretch lace, 1 inch wide, for straps
nylon lingerie *or* polyester thread

TOOLS NEEDED:

pattern paper
scissors
transparent tape
ballpoint pins
#9 ballpoint sewing-machine needle

PROCEDURE:

1. Wash the tricot to preshrink it before you begin working. Then measure your bust and hips to determine your size according to the chart below.

	small	*medium*	*large*
bust	32 inches	34 inches	36 inches
hips	34–36 inches	36–38 inches	38–40 inches

Then enlarge the three pattern pieces to size on the pattern paper (page 17), transfer the pattern markings, cut out the pieces, and label them.

2. Fold the tricot on its lengthwise grain and lay the front and back pattern pieces on the fold, following the markings on the pattern. Make certain that the stretch of the fabric will go around the body. Then cut out. Open up the fabric and lay the bodice front piece on it; cut out. Flip the pattern over, and cut a second bodice front. Mark the right sides of all pieces with transparent tape.

3. Lay out the two bodice front pieces—you should have a right and a left—on a flat surface with their right sides up. With the right side of the nylon lace up, tape the bottom edge of the lace to the top of the bodice fronts so that the top edge of the lace is even with the top edge of the tricot. When you get to the points of the bodice, you

140

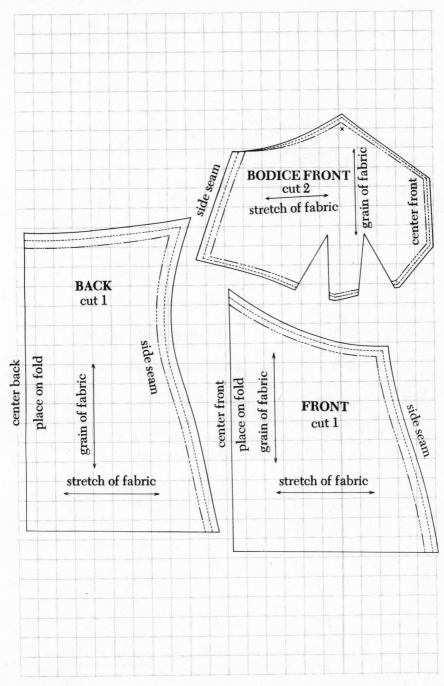

BODICE FRONT
cut 2
stretch of fabric
grain of fabric
center front
side seam

BACK
cut 1
center back
place on fold
grain of fabric
side seam
stretch of fabric

FRONT
cut 1
center front
place on fold
grain of fabric
side seam
stretch of fabric

------ small
·········· medium
―――― large

141

will have to miter the lace to make it fit smoothly. Simply fold the lace back over itself and sew a dart in each side wide enough to take up the excess lace (Diagram 1). Use a narrow zigzag and a short stitch length

Diagram 1

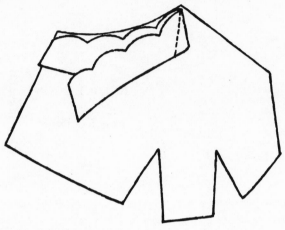

or a short straight stitch. Trim the lace close to the dart. Using a wide zigzag and medium stitch length or a medium straight stitch, topstitch the lace along both the top and the bottom edges. Trim the fabric close to the topstitching at the top edge of the lace only. Apply the lace to the top edge of the back piece in the same way (Diagram 2).

Diagram 2

4. Using the rolled seam technique—a wide zigzag with a short stitch length—or a short straight stitch with a ¼-inch seam, sew the darts in the front bodice, stitching from the bottom to the point of the dart (Diagram 3). Then, with the needle still in the fabric, turn the tricot and sew back a few stitches to lock the stitching in place.

Diagram 3

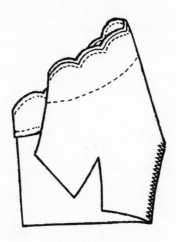

5. With the right sides together, join the two bodice front pieces at the center front, using a rolled seam or a ¼-inch seam allowance with a short straight stitch (Diagram 4).

Diagram 4

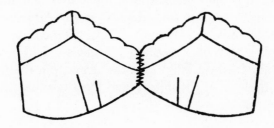

6. Join the bodice to the camisole front, right sides together, by rolling the seam or by sewing it with a short straight stitch and allowing a ¼-inch seam allowance (Diagram 5). Pin it first at the center front and side seams to make the job easier.

Diagram 5

7. With the right sides together, join the front to the back at the side seams, using the rolled seam method or the short straight stitch with a ¼-inch seam allowance. Sew from the bottom to the top, matching the lace at the side edges.

8. To finish the bottom edge of the camisole, stitch ¼ inch from the edge, using a narrow zigzag and short stitch length or a double row of short straight stitching and being careful not to stretch the fabric as you sew. Trim the tricot close to the stitching.

9. To make the straps, cut the stretch lace in half and place one end of each piece under the lace trim on the top edge of the camisole back. The ends should extend under the lace about ½ inch and the straps should be about 3 inches in from the side seams. Attach them by topstitching over them two or three times, using a medium zigzag and a medium stitch length or a medium straight stitch. Then try on the camisole to find the best length for the straps; pin the front ends in place under the lace at the miters, and topstitch them in place.

Chemise Camisole

The chemise camisole is an abbreviated version of the chemise slip in Project 19, having all its virtues plus one— it can be combined with the knee-length half slip in Project 15 or the long half slip in Project 16 to make an elegant contribution to lingerie design, particularly when a beautifully embroidered floral design is added to the bodice and the hemline of the slip. To capture the mysterious look of the East, make both pieces up in silky black, edge them with narrow black lace, and do the embroidery in lacquer reds and blues. For a demure Victorian look, use a rich ivory or bone fabric with ecru lace, and work the embroidery in muted pinks and soft greens. If spaghetti straps were to be substituted for the stretch lace, this ensemble could easily be moved out into a starry evening.

MATERIALS NEEDED:

½ yard nylon tricot, 45 inches wide
1 yard nylon lace, 1 to 2 inches wide
1 yard stretch lace, 1 inch wide, for straps
nylon lingerie *or* polyester thread

TOOLS NEEDED:

pattern paper
scissors
transparent tape
ballpoint pins
#9 ballpoint sewing-machine needle

PROCEDURE:

1. Since the chemise camisole is very much like the chemise slip in Project 19, follow the steps in that project for enlarging the pattern but cut it off at the camisole line.

2. Construct the camisole by following steps 2 through 6 but omit the lace on the bottom edge. Instead, stitch about ¼ inch up from the bottom edge, using a narrow zigzag and short stitch length or a double row of short straight stitching. Trim the tricot close to the stitching.

3. To make the stretch-lace straps, cut the lace in half and place one end of each length behind the back lace, at the x. The ends should just touch the tricot underneath. Using a wide zigzag and medium stitch length or a medium straight stitch, topstitch across the strap at the bottom and top edges of the lace to hold it in place. Then try on the camisole to determine the best length for the straps; pin the front ends under the lace on the front above the points of the darts. Topstitch in place as you did for the back and trim away any extra length.

Project 23

Peasant Camisole

This front-laced eyelet-trimmed camisole is an updated, undies version of the sometimes gay, sometimes subdued vests worn by the gypsies with full-sleeved shirts and voluminous skirts. This same style was also standard dress for the peasant people of Portugal, Spain, and the Balkan countries. In America, it was daily wear for the women of the frontier. Although this style has moved in and out of fashion's limelight, it has always been an appealing style and one that seems here to stay. Happily, it is also one well-suited for undies, particularly in combination with the ruffled peasant petticoat in Project 17. Both could be made in a cotton flannel and worn as outer wear—with or without the full-sleeved shirt. Of course, the earthy simplicity of the camisole is enough to enable it to stand all on its own.

MATERIALS NEEDED:

1 yard batiste, Indian gauze, *or* broadcloth
   (combination cotton and polyester), 36 to 45 inches wide
2/3 yard eyelet lace, 3 inches wide, for front bodice
3 yards polyester-cotton lace trim, ⅜ inch wide
2 buttons, ½ inch in diameter
1 hood drawstring with needlepoint tip *or* ⅛-inch-diameter
   cable cord, approximately 4 feet long
polyester thread

TOOLS NEEDED:

pattern paper
scissors
straight pins
#9 sewing-machine needle

PROCEDURE:

1. Wash the fabric to preshrink it. Measure your bust to determine your size according to the chart below.

small	*medium*	*large*
32 inches	34 inches	36 inches

Enlarge to size the five pattern pieces on the pattern paper (page 17), transfer any pattern markings, cut out the pieces, and label them.

2. Fold the fabric in half on the lengthwise grain and lay the back yoke and back bodice on the fold, following the pattern markings. Lay the remaining pieces on the remaining folded fabric. Cut out the pieces.

3. Cut two pieces of eyelet to the same length as the center front edge of the bodice front. Lay one section of the eyelet, right side up, on the right side of the front edge of one front bodice piece so that the eyelet overlaps the edge by about ½ inch. (If only one edge of the eyelet is scalloped, be sure to place that edge at the center front so that the drawstring can be run through the holes in the scallops. Turn under the unscalloped edge about ¼ inch and press.) Topstitch

each square = 1 inch

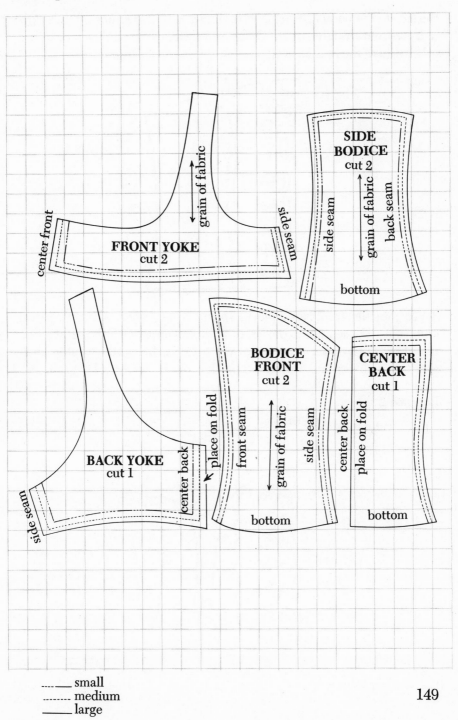

FRONT YOKE
cut 2

center front

grain of fabric

side seam

SIDE BODICE
cut 2

side seam

grain of fabric

back seam

bottom

BACK YOKE
cut 1

side seam

center back

place on fold

BODICE FRONT
cut 2

front seam

grain of fabric

side seam

bottom

CENTER BACK
cut 1

center back
place on fold

bottom

------ small
------ medium
------ large

149

the lace to the bodice, using a wide zigzag with a medium stitch length or a medium straight stitch (Diagram 1). Repeat to add the lace to the other side of the bodice front.

Diagram 1

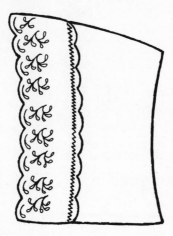

4. To join the front yoke pieces to the front bodice sections, place one front yoke section to one front bodice section with the right sides together. Turn under the edge of the yoke at the center front so that about ¾ inch extends beyond the edge of the eyelet (Diagram 2).

Diagram 2

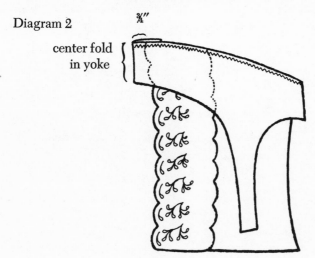

Begin sewing at the center front fold of the yoke extension, easing the yoke and the bodice to fit smoothly. Sew with a narrow zigzag and a short stitch length or a short straight stitch and allow a ¼-inch seam. Repeat this procedure for the other side of the bodice. The extensions on each side will accommodate the buttons and buttonholes. When the garment is turned right side out, it should look like Diagram 3.

Diagram 3

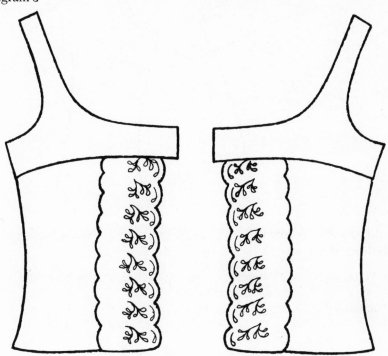

5. With right sides together, join the bodice side sections to the center back bodice piece, sewing ¼-inch seams and using either a narrow zigzag with a short stitch length or a short straight stitch. (The zigzag is a better choice as it will finish the seam and prevent raveling.)

6. With your machine still set for the same stitch, attach the back yoke to the back bodice, right sides together and with a ¼-inch seam. Use the same procedure to join the shoulder seams.

7. Place the narrow lace trim around the edge of each armhole. The

right side of the lace should be up and it should be applied to the right side of the armhole fabric (Diagram 4). The trim should over-

Diagram 4

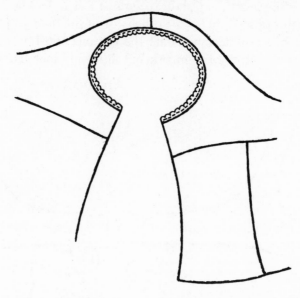

lap the yoke by about ¼ inch. Topstitch, using a wide zigzag with a medium stitch length or a medium straight stitch.

8. With right sides together, join the front of the camisole to the

Diagram 5

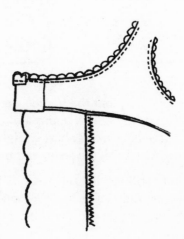

back at the side seams. Stitch with a narrow zigzag and a short stitch length or a short straight stitch with a ¼-inch seam allowance.

9. Add the narrow lace trim to the neckline in the same way as described for the armhole in step 7. On each side of the center front, turn the end of the lace around to the wrong side of the yoke about ½ inch and sew in place when you come to it (Diagram 5).

10. To hem the bottom of the camisole, turn under ¼ inch of fabric, press, turn under another ¼ inch, and press again. Then topstitch, using a wide zigzag with a medium stitch length or a medium straight stitch.

11. Make two buttonholes on the right-side extension of the front yoke. Mark the positions for the buttons on the left-side yoke extension and sew on (Diagram 6). Lace the drawstring through the eyelet holes starting either at the top or the bottom of the camisole.

Diagram 6

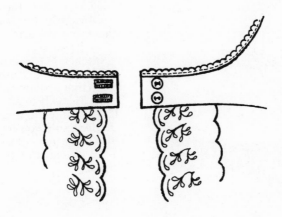

Project 24

Crocheted Victorian Valentine Undies

Filet lace is a crochet technique used by the Victorians to create "pictures" on an open mesh background. The mesh is created by a simple double crochet–chain 1 stitch. Each square on the graph represents an open square on the crocheted piece. Where a square is filled in, work a double crochet in the chain-1 space between double crochets on the row below, to fill in the crocheted square. Obviously, you needn't be an expert crocheter to work up this unique project— all you need to know are the basic stitches. We've made our undies in a smashing red to complement the heart design that's been worked in, but they'd be just as lovely in an ecru or a jet black. If you wanted to transform them into a bathing suit, you could line the pieces with a color that either matches the yarn or strongly contrasts with it.

MATERIALS NEEDED:

3 balls (1 ounce each) Bucilla Paradise, in bright red
E crochet hook *or* size to obtain gauge
3 yards narrow grosgrain ribbon, approximately ½ inch wide

Gauge: 8 squares = 3 inches

Abbreviations: ch . . . . chain
                 sc . . . . single crochet
                 dc . . . . double crochet
                 sl st . . . slip stitch
                 rnd . . . round

Note: Fits small and medium sizes.

PROCEDURE:

PANTY: Row 1: Ch 75, sc in 2nd ch from hook, sc in every ch across. Row 2: Turn, ch 4, dc in 2nd sc, *ch 1, skip 1 sc, dc in next sc. Repeat from * across—37 squares, 38 dc's. Row 3: Ch 4, dc in next dc, *ch 1, dc in next dc. *At the same time,* begin working filet pattern, beginning at top of Graph 1. Repeat from * across. Row 4: Repeat row 3, working next row of filet pattern. Row 5: Ch 3, dc into 2nd dc, work mesh and pattern across to 3rd dc from end, dc in last dc (decrease made on each side of panty). Rows 6–16: Continue to decrease at each edge and to work filet mesh pattern. When pattern has been completed, work open mesh squares only. At row 16, you should have 15 squares. Row 17: Ch 1, sc in 1st space, *sc in each dc and ch-1 space across, ending sc in last space—27 sc's. Rows 18–27: Ch 1, sc in 2nd sc, sc across; skip 2nd sc from end, sc in last sc (decrease made at each edge). Rows 28–41: Work even in sc across 8 stitches. Rows 42–59: Working in sc, increase at each edge by working 2 sc's in first and last stitches. Row 60: Ch 4, dc in 4th ch from hook, *ch 1, skip 1 sc, dc in next sc. Repeat from * across, ending dc in last sc, ch 1, dc in last sc (increase made at each edge)—24 squares, 25 dc's. Row 61: Ch 4, dc in 4th ch from hook, *ch 1, dc in next dc. Repeat from * across, ending dc in last dc, ch 1, dc in last dc. Rows 62–66: Work as row 61, increasing at each edge. *At the same time,* work filet pattern, from the bottom of Graph 2 up. Rows 67–68: Work as above, but do not increase at edges. Row 69: Work mesh only. Row 70: Ch 1, sc into ch-1 space; sc in each dc and ch-1 space across. Break off. Sew side seams from top edge to beginning of leg curve.

LEG EDGE: Work 1 row sc around leg opening; sl st to beg ch-1; ch 3, sc into 3rd ch from hook, sc into next sc (picot made), sc into each of next 2 sc's. Repeat from * around, to beginning of sc rows on bikini, sc into each sc to end of sc rows, then repeat from * to end of round. Join with sl st and break off.

TOP EDGE: Rnd 1: Join yarn at a seam, ch 3, dc into each of next 2 sc's, *ch 1, skip 1 sc, dc into each of next 3 sc's. Repeat from * around; join with sl st to top of beg ch-3. Rnd 2: Ch 1, sc in next stitch, *ch 3, sc into 3rd ch from hook, sc into each of next 3 stitches. Repeat from * around, working sc's into each dc and ch-1 space. Break off.

FINISHING: Weave ends in. Thread narrow grosgrain ribbon through top dc row; tie in front.

BRA (make 2): Row 1: Ch 40, sc in 2nd ch from hook, sc across. Row 2: Ch 4, *skip 1 sc, dc in next sc, ch 1. Repeat from * across, ending dc in last sc. Rows 3–12: Follow Graph 3 for filet mesh pattern, beginning at bottom of chart on row 3 (row 4 on your work), begin decreasing at each edge (see row 5, panty) on row 5. Row 13: Ch 1, sc into top of final dc square, sc around outside edge of bra, working 3 sc's into each corner stitch. End with sl st into top of beg ch-1, then ch 60 for tie; break off.

FINISHING: Thread ribbon through squares of bottom mesh row; tie ends into bow in front, adjusting bra to fit around rib cage.

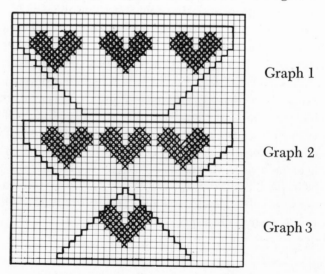

Graph 1

Graph 2

Graph 3

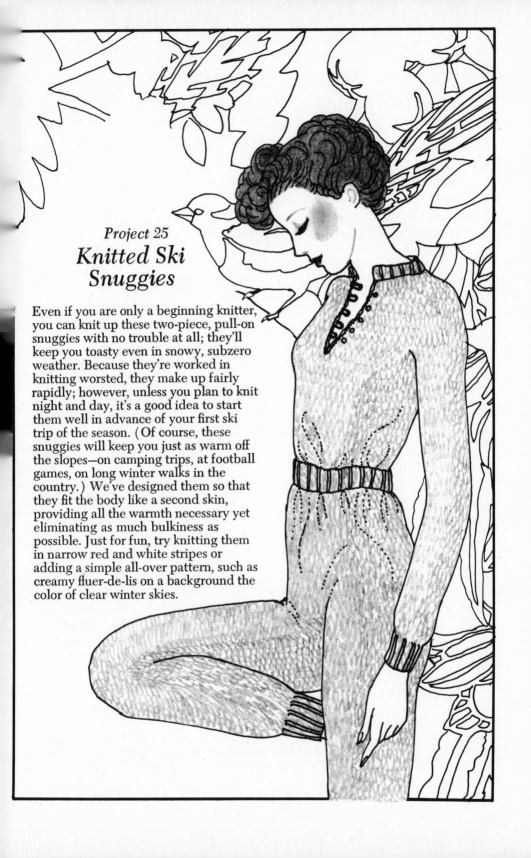

Project 25
Knitted Ski Snuggies

Even if you are only a beginning knitter,
you can knit up these two-piece, pull-on
snuggies with no trouble at all; they'll
keep you toasty even in snowy, subzero
weather. Because they're worked in
knitting worsted, they make up fairly
rapidly; however, unless you plan to knit
night and day, it's a good idea to start
them well in advance of your first ski
trip of the season. (Of course, these
snuggies will keep you just as warm off
the slopes—on camping trips, at football
games, on long winter walks in the
country.) We've designed them so that
they fit the body like a second skin,
providing all the warmth necessary yet
eliminating as much bulkiness as
possible. Just for fun, try knitting them
in narrow red and white stripes or
adding a simple all-over pattern, such as
creamy fluer-de-lis on a background the
color of clear winter skies.

MATERIALS NEEDED:

knitting worsted:
  tops—16 ounces
  bottoms—28 (28, 30) ounces
#5 circular knitting needles, 29 inches long
1 set #5 double-pointed knitting needles
E crochet hook
approximately 1 yard elastic, 1 inch wide
5 buttons

Gauge: 5 stitches = 1 inch
        15 rows = 2 inches

ABBREVIATIONS:

k . . . knit
p . . . purl
inc . . . increase
dec . . . decrease
psso . . . pass slip stitch over
st . . . stitch
tog . . . together
dp . . . double-pointed

MEASUREMENTS:

	small		medium		large	
bust	32	inches	34	inches	36	inches
waist	23½	inches	25½	inches	27½	inches
hips	34	inches	36	inches	38	inches
thighs	19	inches	21	inches	23	inches
ankles	7	inches	8	inches	9	inches

PROCEDURE:

TOP: *Body:* With #5 circular needles, cast on 122 (132, 142) sts. Work in ribbing k 2, p 2 for 2 inches. Mark sides, dividing body equally into front and back halves. Inc 1 st each side of marker every inch

158

10 times (this will be an inc of 4 sts per inc row). Work even on these 162 (172, 182) sts until piece measures 12 (14, 14) inches (or measured distance from 2 inches below waist to underarm). Divide for arms: Bind off 9 (10, 11) sts after each marker. At this point, front and back will be worked separately—k 1 row, p 1 row—on 2 double-pointed needles. To prevent your work from slipping off the needles, wrap the ends with rubber bands or use commercially available rubber stops. Place the 72 (76, 80) sts for the front on a holder. *Back:* With inside of work facing you, p 1 row. Next row k 2, k 2 tog, k to last 4 sts, slip 1 st, k 1, psso, k 2. Repeat these 2 dec rows 24 (26, 28) times. Place the remaining 22 sts on holder. *Front:* Work the above 2 dec rows 6 times (60, 64, 68 sts). Divide for front opening: Place half these 60 (64, 68) sts on holder. Work on remaining 30 (32, 34) sts—k 1 row, p 1 row—continuing to dec 1 st every knit row on outer edges until 11 sts remain. Place these sts on holder. Work opposite side in similar fashion. *Sleeves:* Using dp needles, cast on 28 (34, 38) sts. Join and work in ribbing k 2, p 2 for 2 inches. Place marker for underarm seam at join. Inc 6 sts across next row. Inc 1 st at each side of dividing marker every inch until 60 (66, 70) sts remain. Work even until piece measures 18 inches (or desired length from wrist to 2 inches below shoulder). Repeat for other sleeve. *Raglan cap: (Note:* Open at marker so that raglan will be worked k 1 row, p 1 row on 2 dp needles.) Bind off 4 (5, 5) sts at the beginning of the next 2 rows. Dec each side of needle on k rows as for front and back until 6 sts remain. Place these sts on a holder. Repeat for other raglan cap. *Neckband:* Pick up 70 (75, 80) sts around neck, leaving the opening in front. K 2, p 2 in ribbing for 1 inch. Bind off. *Finishing:* Crochet border, in chain st, along edge of neck opening. Attach 5 crocheted loops to close front. Stitch sleeves to body and sew on buttons.

BOTTOMS: *Waistband:* Using #5 circular needles, cast on 130 (140, 150) sts. Mark sides, dividing piece equally into front and back halves. K for 1 inch, p 1 row, k another inch, p 1 row. *Body:* Inc 1 st each side of marker every ½ inch 10 times (this will be an inc of 4 sts per inc row). Work even on these 170 (180, 190) sts until piece measures 8 (9, 10) inches (or measured distance from waist to crotch). In next row, place the middle 15 sts from the front and the middle 15 sts from the back on holders. The body has now been divided into left and right legs, which will be worked separately. *Legs:* Place the 70 (75, 80) sts of left (or right) leg on dp needles and join by casting on 24 (29, 34) sts (94, 104, 114 sts). Dec 1 st each side of marker every inch 24 (25, 26) times (this will be a dec of 2 sts per inch, as there is only 1 marker on each leg). Continue on these 46 (54, 62) sts until 2 inches less than measured distance from crotch to ankle. In next row, k 2 tog 4 (6, 10) times across row (42, 48, 52 sts). K 2, p 2 in ribbing for 2 inches. Bind off. Repeat for other leg. *Crotch:* Pick up the 15 sts from front holder. K 1 row, p 1 row for 3 inches, decreasing 1 st each side of needle every ½ inch 4 (3, 3) times (7, 9, 9 sts). Bind off. Work same from back holder. *Finishing:* Cut elastic to desired waist size and join ends. Fold top 1 inch of waistband over elastic and stitch down. Join ends of crotch and attach to legs.